The Bread Machine Cookbook

Fuss-Free Recipes for Making Homemade Bread
with Any Bread Maker

Daniella Gallagher

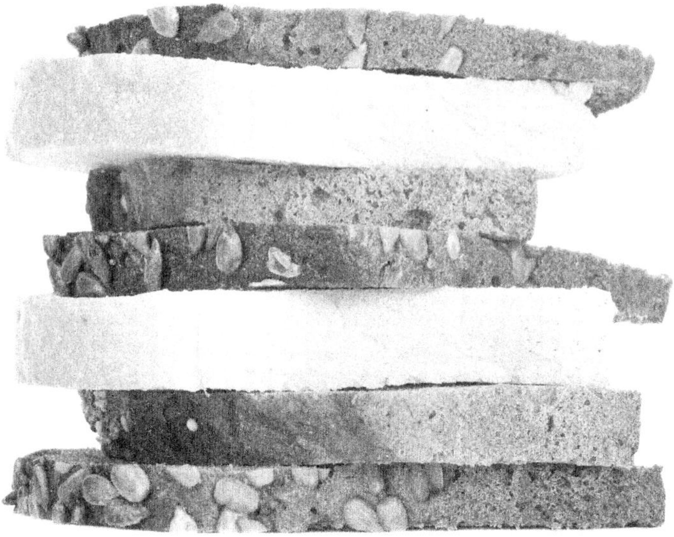

© Copyright 2020 Daniella Gallagher
All rights reserved.

The content contained within this book may not be reproduced, duplicated or transmitted without direct written permission from the author or the publisher.

Under no circumstances will any blame or legal responsibility be held against the publisher, or author, for any damages, reparation, or monetary loss due to the information contained within this book. Either directly or indirectly. You are responsible for your own choices, actions, and results.

Legal Notice:

This book is copyright protected. This book is only for personal use. You cannot amend, distribute, sell, use, quote or paraphrase any part, or the content within this book, without the consent of the author or publisher.

Disclaimer Notice:

Please note the information contained within this document is for educational and entertainment purposes only. All effort has been executed to present accurate, up to date, and reliable, complete information. No warranties of any kind are declared or implied. Readers acknowledge that the author is not engaging in the rendering of legal, financial, medical or professional advice. The content within this book has been derived from various sources. Please consult a licensed professional before attempting any techniques outlined in this book.

By reading this document, the reader agrees that under no circumstances is the author responsible for any losses, direct or indirect, which are incurred as a result of the use of the information contained within this document, including, but not limited to, — errors, omissions, or inaccuracies.

CONTENTS

- INTRODUCTION 7
- CHAPTER 1: MAIN INGREDIENTS 9
- CHAPTER 2: BREAD MACHINE CYCLES 14
- CHAPTER 3: THINGS TO KEEP IN MIND 18
  - Ingredients - Order of Addition 18
  - Exceeding The Bread Machine's Capacity 18
  - Measuring Ingredients 19
  - About Yeast 20
  - Consistency Is Key 20
  - Write Things Down 21
  - Get The Most out of Your Machine 21
- CHAPTER 4: HOW TO STORE BREAD 22
  - How to Store Dough 23
  - Freezing Dough 24
  - Freezing Pizza Dough and Bread Rolls 25
  - Freezing The Finished Product 26
- CHAPTER 5: TROUBLESHOOTING 27
- CHAPTER 6: CLASSIC BREADS 30
  - Country-Styled White Bread 30
  - Honey and Milk White Bread 32
  - Butter Bread 34
  - Basic White Bread 36
  - 50/50 Bread 38
  - Classic French Bread 40
  - Sourdough 42
- CHAPTER 7: WHOLE-WHEAT BREADS 44
  - Whole Wheat Bread 44
  - Whole Wheat and Honey Bread 46
  - Whole Wheat Seeds and Syrup Bread 48
  - 100% Whole Wheat Bread 50

Seeded Whole Wheat Bread 52
Honey and Oatmeal Whole Wheat Bread 54

CHAPTER 8: CHEESE & ITALIAN STYLED BREADS 56

Close-Grained Cheddar Cheese Bread 56
Olive Bread 58
Garlic and Herb Bread 60
Italian Parmesan Bread 62
Pepperoni and Cheese Bread 64
Quick Bake Italian Bread 66
Ciabatta 68
Bacon and Cheese Bread 70
Spiced Jalapeno Cheese Bread 72

CHAPTER 9: NUT & SEED BREADS 74

Rye Bread with Caraway 74
Sunflower and Flax Seed Bread 76
Sweet Mixed Nut Bread 78
Multigrain Sandwich Loaf 80
Simple and Savory Mixed Seed Loaf 82
Nut Bread 84
Almond and Dates Sweet Bread 86

CHAPTER 10: SPECIAL BREADS 88

Gluten-Free Bread 88
No Salt Added White Bread 90
Quinoa Bread 92
Low-Carb Keto Bread 94
Paleo and Dairy-Free Bread 96

CHAPTER 11: FRUITY BREADS & CAKE 98

Raisin Bread 98
Orange Cake Loaf 100
Fruity Harvest Bread 102
Eggless Vanilla Loaf 104
Mardi Gras King Cake 106
Banana Bread 108
Apple Cake 110

Coffee Cake 112

CHAPTER 12: ROLLS & PIZZA **114**

"Po Boy" Rolls from New Orleans 114
100% Whole Wheat Dinner Rolls 116
classic Dinner Rolls.. 118
Vegan Dinner Rolls 120
Buttery Dinner Rolls... 122
Cinnamon Rolls 124
Pizza Dough Recipe 127

CHAPTER 13: ASSORTED PARTY RECIPES............................. **130**

Breadsticks.. 130
Texas Roadhouse-Style Glazed Buns 132
Chocolate Chip Banana Bread 134
Cranberry and Cardamom Bread 136
Chocolate Chip Brioche.. 138

CONCLUSION **140**

INTRODUCTION

Often, we purchase an item, and we may have gotten good use from it, but then the novelty eventually wears off. I can guarantee you that this book will revive your love for that bread maker or inspire you to put your brand new one to work if you haven't already begun baking.

Bread is an everyday staple. A food item we regularly purchase, buying store-bought bread is undoubtedly convenient. However, store-bought bread is packed with chemical additives, extra sugars, and salts to ensure longer shelf life. To gauge how baking your own bread is worth it, do yourself a favor; look at the label on the back of store-bought bread and compare it to the list of ingredients needed to make your own. You will notice the stark contrast of ingredients. Store-bought includes emulsifiers and agents, but a basic bread recipe is made up of very few affordable ingredients, none of which include words that I even struggle pronouncing. And when you take a step back and look at the bigger picture, you'll see you are better off baking your own bread, especially with quite a convenient and useful tool, such as a bread machine.

There are many pros to making bread at home, including the fact that it is far tastier than your standard, mass-produced bread. You can alter ingredients, meaning you have more control over the sugar, fiber, Protein: and salt content. You can also get creative by adding in nuts and dried fruits. Buying your own ingredients means you can manage all of what goes in the machine and provides you the opportunity of seeking the freshest ingredients.

Home-baked bread always contains more nutrients, and for those who have allergies, baking your own bread can help you manage what gets included versus trusting what a store-bought bread promises in terms of it being nut-free, dairy-free, or gluten-free.

Another plus point, and something I personally love, is that by making your own bread, you can make bread for any occasion. You can even bake a cake in a bread maker! During the festive season, you see plenty of specially crafted bread in stores, but they come with a hefty price tag. Making your own is a sure-fire way to get the family involved, save money, and create a newfound tradition.

I come from a big family myself, and bread has always been part of my daily life. Even now, my husband and kids beg me to bake their favorites a few times a week. Some days I am surprised with the lasting capacity of my bread maker, and I hope that you and your family will feel the same once you have sampled some of the recipes I have collected and included in this book.

I have also thrown in a few informative bits which will answer any questions you may have if your loaf of bread comes out looking or tasting differently from what you had imagined. We are all human, and there is nothing more frustrating than not knowing the answer to a burning question. The bread cycles mentioned in the book should also help to figure out which one to use when baking different loaves of bread.

Baking bread is my passion, and creating recipes and sampling new ones is an essential part of my life. Spending time as a professional baker for the last 17 years means I can promise you that baking your own bread is 100% worth it.

The bread recipes that you will find on these pages have been baked by myself to celebrate anniversaries, birthdays, and special occasions. Many of my friends and family members have also rushed out to buy a bread maker upon seeing how easy it is and, of course, twisting my arm to share a few secret recipes, which are also included in this book.

Do not be intimidated by your bread maker! The recipes are there to show you how easy it can be to create mouthwatering loaves of bread. Better yet, I have included recipes for one pound, one and a half pounds, and two pounds of sliced bread. There are also nutrition facts per slice for the conscious eater.

Start baking today, and you'll see how easy it is to put a loaf of fresh homemade bread on the table. And above all, there's nothing better than the smell of a fresh bread baking or tucking into a slice straight from out of the oven. Who can resist that?

CHAPTER 1:

MAIN INGREDIENTS

You only need four ingredients to make a great loaf of bread with a bread machine:

- Yeast Flour
- Liquid (typically, water or milk)
- Salt

Now, let's get into more detail about these ingredients to have a better understanding of each of them and what they do in the process.

FLOUR

Flour is the main ingredient for any bread product. The type of flour you choose will make a difference in the loaf you bake. And when it comes to choosing flour, there are so many types it can be overwhelming. But what you need to pay attention to is the amount of protein in the flour: the higher the flour's protein content, the bigger the flours gluten-forming potential in the dough. And gluten in bread is the structure that holds the loaf together and gives bread its unique texture.

Which flour to use?

There are five main varieties of flour used when baking bread.

- *All-purpose flour* contains up to 12% gluten and is ideal for use in most baked goods. Try to get unbleached options for baking bread (unbleached indicates that the flour has not been chemically treated to be whitened).

- *Whole wheat flour* is more abundant in nutrients because it includes some of the grain's germ and bran. Always check the packing of the flour to ensure it is 100% whole wheat and not blended with anything else. It gives off very nutty flavors, making it ideal for nut and seed loaves or traditional whole wheat bread. This particular flour contains up to 13% gluten. Whole wheat flour creates denser loaves with more natural textures, and when baked, tends to have a chewy crust.

- *Bread flour* will be your go-to flour when making bread unless the recipe stipulates otherwise. It contains roughly 14% gluten and provides the baker with a more pliable dough, which in turn creates a lighter bread. Most times, all-purpose flour may be substituted with bread flour, but note that it may require more liquid because of the gluten percentage.

- *White whole wheat flour* is a flour that is relatively new to the market. It is created using white spring wheat that is sweeter than standard wheat varieties and is lighter in color. It has a gluten percentage of 12%. It may be useful when wanting to substitute all-purpose flour with a healthier option. It also has a mild taste, which is great when you wish to add herbs or other flavors to your bread.

- *Rye flour* is milled from whole rye grains, berries, or grass. Rye flour improves the nutritional content of bread loaves. Traditionally, rye flour is used to make rye or sourdough bread. Rye flours may come in three varieties: light, medium, and dark. The lighter they are, the less bran has been left in the flour after production. The darker the rye flour is, the more bran has been left behind. Darker rye is more nutritious and flavorful than lighter rye. Because rye flour doesn't have the same gluten as other flours (in fact, it contains a different protein structure altogether), it has to be mixed with all-purpose or bread flour. Otherwise, the loaf will be dense.

YEAST

Yeast is a key ingredient that makes bread expand and become softer and lighter. Yeast is what allows all baked goods to rise. Yeast quickly absorbs moisture, causing it to turn sugar and starch into carbon dioxide. The small bubbles of gas allow the dough to grow and increase in size.

What kind of yeast to use?

Bread machine yeast (also known as rapid-rise yeast) and instant dry yeast become active a lot faster than active dry yeast and are better suited for use in a bread machine. You can use active dry yeast in a bread machine as well (in fact, you'll notice some recipes in this cookbook call for exactly active dry yeast); however, active dry yeast is not recommended for one-hour or express cycles, as it needs more time to activate.

Additionally, I would recommend that you only buy yeast when you need it and suggest that you use a new packet every time you plan to bake something. Yeast is a very temperamental product and makes for difficult storing because air changes its ability to work effectively.

If you want to substitute instant or bread machine yeast for active dry yeast, use 25% less instant yeast than active dry.

LIQUID (TYPICALLY WATER, MILK, OR POWDER MILK MIXED IN WITH WATER)

The liquid in the dough is one of the main ingredients responsible for activating all the items within your dough mixture. It dissolves the yeast and salt, hydrates the starch and the proteins. The liquid is accountable for the consistency of the dough.

The temperature of the liquid you use for baking bread is critical.

Remember, the yeast that makes the bread rise is a living organism. If you use water that is too hot, there's a risk of killing the yeast. If you use liquid that is too cold, the yeast will not activate properly. A common rule of thumb is to use lukewarm water or any other liquid.

You can use water directly from the tap, but if you suspect your tap water is too hard or high in chlorine, then try using bottled water.

SALT

Many people question the necessity of salt in bread baking. The short answer to that is yes, it's necessary. Bread without salt would be bland, and it will not allow other ingredients and aromas to sing. Also, salt plays as an inhibitor to the yeast in the bread dough. It slows the rising process of the dough, which gives the gluten enough time to strengthen and develop, resulting in a better crust and a better crumb. Not to mention, it adds to the flavor of the bread. Without salt, a basic loaf is going to taste bland, flat, and somewhat papery.

All recipes in this book call for sea salt, but you can use whatever you already have in your home.

OIL / BUTTER

Oil has numerous functions when it comes to baking, and that includes carrying the flavors, extending the freshness of the baked goods, and enhancing the texture. Oil also helps when it comes to the kneading process, making the dough more pliable and easier to work with.

Using extra-virgin olive oil in place of standard vegetable oil is a good choice as it carries with it numerous health benefits.

Butter holds many properties which include, adding flavor, improving the shelf-life of the product, keeping bread moist, and promoting a richer texture.

Softened butter is best, as it allows the bread maker to churn the ingredients and create a smoother dough. Never use butter straight from out of the refrigerator without letting it soften first. A faster way to do so is to place it in the microwave for a very short period of time. Or you can simply leave the butter out of the refrigerator to reach room temperature.

SUGAR

Sugar is not an essential ingredient in bread baking. You can make basic everyday bread with a long rising time without any sweeteners. However, apart from its sweetening effect on cakes and bakes, sugar does have an important role to play in the baking process.

It can be simply explained. As you probably already know, the process of the dough rising and expanding is called fermentation. It's when the yeast eats the sugar in the dough and develops gases which fill the dough with air, achieving soft and fluffy bread in the end.

Today, because the baking process has been shortened, in some recipes adding a little bit of sugar can help during the fermentation of the dough: sugar feeds the yeast, resulting in a faster rise. It doesn't have to be refined sugar. If a recipe requires sugar, feel free to substitute it with a healthier option, for example:

- Honey
- Maple syrup
- Molasses

CHAPTER 2:
BREAD MACHINE CYCLES

Bread machines are a fantastic kitchen accessory to own.

These small compact wonders have many options and settings for baking an assortment of bread masterfully. Once you become familiar with your bread machine's settings, the chance to create and experiment is endless.

It is essential to know what each setting on your machine can deliver, making it easier to understand what function to use when it is time to bake your loaf. Being on a first-name basis with your bread machine will allow you to create flavorsome bread, making you wish that you had purchased the machine sooner!

Bread machines can come in two different varieties. Some brands hold specific settings that you cannot alter, so it is wise to follow the instruction manual when making different styles of bread to see which setting will be ideal.

Whereas some bread machines come with basic settings with times and programming that you can alter. For instance, if you notice that the bread did not rise as you hoped for, you can extend the rising time. By allowing you to change some of the settings to suit your needs, you can create the perfect loaf of bread.

Now, let me help you understand the various cycles and settings that you can find on your bread machine.

BASIC CYCLE

This setting is the most commonly used function of the bread machine, allowing you to create standard bread. This function generally runs for three to four hours, depending on the loaf size and style of bread. You can also use this setting when making bread using whole wheat flour.

SWEET BREAD CYCLE

This cycle, as the name suggests, is for bread that has higher sugar or fat content than standard bread. The setting is also used when ingredients such as cheese and eggs are used. This function allows the bread to bake at a lower temperature than other functions as the ingredients included may cause the crust to burn or darken in color.

NUT OR RAISIN CYCLE

Though you can add ingredients such as nuts and dried fruit pieces into your pan, some machines tend to churn them too finely. The nut or raisin cycle is there to ensure that these ingredients stay relatively chunky, adding texture and sweetness to the bread. This function is ideal as it alerts the baker when it's time to add in the nuts or fruit pieces.

WHOLE WHEAT CYCLE

Whole wheat bread needs to be kneaded and churned longer than your standard loaves. That is why this cycle is perfect for bread that calls for this type of flour to be used. This function allows the bread to rise high enough and stops it from becoming too dense.

French Bread Cycle

The majority of the bread from the Mediterranean regions such as Italy or France come out far better when using this function rather than the basic cycle. Many French styled loaves of bread hold none to very little sugar. Bread from these regions needs a longer rising time and a lower and longer temperature. This is so that it can create the textures and crusts we have grown to love and savor.

Dough Cycle

This cycle is perfect for making pizza doughs and doughs used for making dinner rolls. The machine will mix and knead your ingredients, allowing you to then remove the dough, add your desired toppings or fillings, and then continue to bake them in your conventional oven. This saves you from having to knead the dough yourself and leaves little cleaning afterward, which is a big win for everyone.

This cycle can also be used for making cookie dough, flatbreads, breadsticks, and pie crusts.

Rapid Bake Cycle

This is for those who make use of quick rise yeast in their bread recipes. The rapid cycle can take anywhere between 30 minutes to two hours of the basic bread cycle, saving you plenty of time. Note that the rapid bake cycle does vary from machine to machine.

Cake or Quick Cycle

This cycle is ideal for recipes that contain no yeast, such as cakes. This a primary cycle to consider when making the store-bought cake and bread mixes. The bread machine does not knead the ingredients together like the other cycles. All it does is mixes the ingredients and bakes it. This cycle and baking time can also vary from one machine to the other.

Jam Cycle

Though bread is delicious served fresh from the bread machine, there is nothing quite as enjoyable as a warm slice of bread served with warm strawberry jam, one of my simple pleasures in life!

A jam cycle on a bread machine is an absolute treat. Quick tip, remember to finely dice your fruit before adding it into the bread machine for the best results. You can have a fresh pot of jam ready within one hour.

TIME-BAKE OR DELAYED CYCLE

This is a novel setting that some bread machines have. It allows you to add the ingredients into the bread machine, then programs it to start baking at a time suited to you. This is a smart and useful function – thanks to it, there have been many days when the house has been awoken to the smell of fresh bread baking.

Word to the wise, bread that has milk or eggs as part of their ingredients should only be delayed for one to two hours to reduce issues with food-borne bacteria.

CRUST FUNCTIONALITY

The crust functionality on bread machines allows the user to select their crust of choice when making bread. Generally, there are three settings for a crust: Soft, medium, and dark. A soft crust is always great, paired with white bread varieties. If you prefer a crispier crust, then the medium and dark crusts will appeal to you. If your bread contains sweeteners, nuts, and grains, it may cause the bread to brown faster. Thus, a light crust setting is recommended. If your machine does not allow you to select a crust function, it means that the option is automatically set when making specific loaves of bread.

CHAPTER 3:
THINGS TO KEEP IN MIND

The process of baking bread with a bread machine is the same as making bread by hand. The significant difference between the two is that the machine does all the mixing, rising, and baking. That's the beauty of having a bread maker - it does all the hands-on work for you. All you have to do is load the machine with the right ingredients, go about your day, and have a beautiful loaf ready to be eaten in quite a short period of time. In this chapter, we will discuss a few essential points to keep in mind when it comes to baking bread with a bread maker.

INGREDIENTS - ORDER OF ADDITION

This is something I cannot stress enough: always add the ingredients to the bread machine in the order that is listed in the recipe or follow your bread machine's user manual. Many of the bread machines have their own way in which they recommend you add the various ingredients. With some bread makers, the dry ingredients should be added first; with others, the wet ingredients go in first. Typically, liquids are added first, then flours and dry ingredients, and lastly, the yeast. That is the way the recipes are constructed. But again, always read your instruction manual and follow its guidelines regarding what to add and the cycle suggested for the type of bread recipe.

EXCEEDING THE BREAD MACHINE'S CAPACITY

All bread machines are created differently. Some bread makers make only 1-pound loaves; others make 1½ or 2-pound loaves. In this book, you'll find most bread recipes for all three options: 1, 1 ½, or 2-pound loaves.

Be careful when adding ingredients so that you do not exceed the capacity of the bread machine. Exceeding capacity can cause the ingredients of either the bread or jam to spill out and over into the rest of the machine, which may damage it. It is also a nightmare to clean if this happens.

Make sure you read your machine's manual to know its features and capacity, and strictly follow its guidelines, especially if you plan on doubling a recipe.

The user manual can also show you how to effectively clean your bread machine and install specific parts such as the paddle or pan.

MEASURING INGREDIENTS

Measure your ingredients correctly and always use the freshest available to you.

The most accurate way to measure dry ingredients is to measure by weight, using a kitchen scale. But not everybody has one. Therefore, to simplify the baking process, all measurements in the recipes are cups and spoons that you already know and use.

However, measuring flour with cups might not be as accurate if not done correctly. Due to the fact that flour settles and compresses during shipping, you might end up with more flour than needed if you dip the measuring cup directly into the flour. To avoid that, what you need to do is aerate the flour in the bag or container every time before measuring it (it also compresses while it's hiding in the back of your cupboard).

Aerating simply means putting air in the flour, making it less compressed. One of the simple and quick ways to aerate your flour is to stir it around with a wooden spoon right in the bag or container you store it in. After you aerate your flour, using a light hand, spoon the flour into the measuring cup, and swipe a knife over the cup to get rid of the excess flour. Don't tap or shake the cup.

Furthermore, always use ingredients, such as eggs or milk, that are at room temperature unless the recipe requires it to be otherwise. Bring your eggs up to room temperature by holding them under warm running water or by leaving them out on the counter for 30 minutes. Heat the milk in the microwave and finely dice room temperature butter before adding them into the bread machine.

If you're using milk powder, I would recommend that you combine the milk powder and water before adding them into bread machines in any recipe that calls for these two ingredients.

ABOUT YEAST

Buying quality yeast will ensure that your bread rises beautifully. Sometimes yeast can lose its strength or become old.

If you have any doubts about the freshness of your yeast and its ability to work properly to deliver delicious bread, I suggest you try the following yeast test to check its activity before using:

Ingredients:

- 2 ¼ tsp yeast
- 1 tsp granulated white sugar
- ½ cup lukewarm water

Directions:

1. Pour the lukewarm water into the measuring cup.
2. Stir in the granulated sugar until it has dissolved.
3. Gently dust the yeast over the top of the water, place the cup in a warm area, and allow it to rest for ten minutes.
4. After the time has elapsed, check on the liquid; if foam has been created and reached the one cup mark, then your yeast is good to go. If there is no foam, or if it hasn't risen, throw away the yeast and use a new yeast packet.

In addition, never place the yeast in direct contact with salt, as this will decrease the activity of the yeast. Use the back of a spoon or your finger to create a small indentation in the top of the flour and place the yeast in the well you created.

CONSISTENCY IS KEY

When your bread machine has mixed the ingredients and formed a dough, be sure to check on its consistency. If the dough appears too dry, add one teaspoon of milk or water to it at a time until the dough is less wet. If the dough seems too wet, add one teaspoon of flour at a time until the dough becomes drier. The perfect dough should be sticky to the touch but not overly dry or wet.

Write Things Down

Keep a notebook and pen handy for when you cook to write down tips and outcomes and what you feel can be excluded or included the next time you bake something. This makes for excellent reference material and can help you avoid future flops. I have been doing this since I was a teenager, dabbling with recipes in the family kitchen with the help of my mother. To this day, I still jot down notes whenever I am baking or trying out new recipes.

Get The Most out of Your Machine

Bread makers are not just for baking bread. You can let your machine make the dough for you and remove it at the end of the kneading cycle and hand form it into a bread loaf, rolls, pizza, or anything else for baking in a traditional oven.

CHAPTER 4:
HOW TO STORE BREAD

Fresh bread, especially those that are considered lean, such as a baguette, ciabatta, and other types that have no or very little sugar and oil content, can only keep for up to two days and no more. However, enriched bread can keep up to 4 to 5 days due to higher fat and sugar content (thanks to eggs, milk, oil, and butter).

Homemade loaves do not have any additives and preservatives to prevent them from growing mold and keep them soft and fresh for many days. Generally, homemade bread should be enjoyed as it is stipulated, fresh.

That leaves many people scratching their heads. Though some people can eat an entire loaf in two days, many others may wonder how you can keep a loaf of homemade bread fresh for longer.

Store-bought bread is engineered to last well past two days for longer shelf life because of all the extra ingredients used like additives and preservatives. Storing fresh bread and keeping it for longer than this time is harder because you are using the freshest of ingredients and adding no chemical extras.

I suggest that you do not place your bread in the refrigerator, hoping that it will keep. Refrigeration changes the texture of the bread completely, leaving it only good for toasting.

A bread box is ideal for storing bread because it allows for enough air to pass through without drying the loaf out and, most importantly, prevents the bread from getting moldy. If you don't have a bread box, wrap the bread in a clean cotton tea towel, then put it in a paper bag. Do not use a plastic bag! Storing homemade bread in plastic bags for longer than a day is not a very good idea. Since plastic doesn't let moisture escape, the bread will become mushy and eventually moldy if there is moisture present. Additionally, I suggest you keep the bread away from direct sunlight: the wrapped loaf will sweat, creating condensation and mold on the loaf.

How to Store Dough

Did you know that all doughs can be popped into the refrigerator?

Store the dough in a greased mixing bowl, making sure the bowl is large enough to accommodate any expansion. Then cover the mixing bowl tightly using plastic wrap before placing it in the refrigerator. The dough can be stored this way for up to 3 days, but I suggest you use it within 48 hours.

Or you can spray the inside of a large zip lock bag with cooking spray (to avoid the dough sticking to the plastic bag), pop the dough in the bag, and then into the refrigerator. That trick will save quite some space in your refrigerator.

When you are ready to use your dough:

1. Place it onto a well-floured surface and knead it for a few minutes (in other words, fold it over itself).

2. Shape the dough into a round boule, place it on a parchment paper, and cover with plastic wrap.
3. Allow it to rest for an hour.
4. Place your Dutch oven in the oven and preheat both to 450°F.
1. Carefully take the pot out of the oven, pick up the parchment paper with the dough, and place it inside the pot.
2. Bake for 30 minutes with a lid on, then remove the lid and bake for another 10 to 15 minutes, or until the crust is golden brown.
3. Let the loaf cool completely before slicing and serving.

FREEZING DOUGH

When you freeze your dough at home, it will take far longer to freeze than the doughs that you have access to at the supermarkets. Manufacturers have freezing systems that freeze the dough very quickly, causing minimal effects on the integrity of the dough and yeast.

Keep in mind that your loaf will not rise as much as it normally would had it been baked right away. That is because some of the yeast in your dough will die during the freezing process. When placing ingredients in your bread maker to create the dough, add 20 to 30% more yeast than the recipe states. This is to compensate for some of the yeast that will die in the freezing process.

Once your dough is ready, let it rise to about double its size, shape it into a round ball and place it in a greased zip lock bag. Don't forget to date the bags. You can store your dough in the freezer for up to 2 weeks.

Once you are ready to bake:

1. Let the dough thaw for 3 hours at room temperature or overnight in the fridge.

2. Then reshape the thawed dough into a round boule and let rise covered with plastic wrap at room temperature for 2 hours, or until bigger in size.

3. Place your Dutch oven in the oven and preheat both to 450°F.

4. Carefully take the pot out of the oven, pick up the parchment paper with the dough, and place it inside the pot.

5. Bake for 30 minutes with a lid on, then remove the lid and bake for another 10 to 15 minutes, or until the crust is golden brown.

6. Let the loaf cool completely before slicing and serving.

FREEZING PIZZA DOUGH AND BREAD ROLLS

When you are ready to freeze your pizza or bread roll dough:

1. Shape into balls for your rolls or flatten the dough into discs for your pizza bases.

2. Place these items on a baking tray lined with parchment, then transfer into the freezer.

3. Remove the tray from the freezer when the dough balls or pizza bases are frozen (can take up to a few hours).

4. Place your dough balls or pizza dough into an airtight freezer bag, and then place them back into the freezer.

5. You can store these in the freezer for up to two weeks.

When you plan to use the doughs, simply remove from the freezer and place it into the refrigerator and allow it to thaw overnight.

For pizza, when ready, remove the thawed base from the refrigerator and the plastic bag, let it rest for about 30 minutes at room temperature, and bake as per recipe instructions.

As for the rolls, the process is quite similar: remove the rolls from the refrigerator and the plastic bag, place them onto a baking tray lined with parchment paper, allow the rolls to rise for about an hour, then bake as per the recipe instructions.

FREEZING THE FINISHED PRODUCT

Freezing already baked bread is a wonderful way to provide a fresh loaf of bread in a very short amount of time.

Once your loaf is ready:

1. Make sure it is cooled completely. This will prevent it from becoming moldy and soggy.

2. Optional: Slice the bread. You can skip this step, but it's quite convenient: instead of thawing the entire loaf, you can only take the slices you'd like to use each time.

3. Double package the bread. Firstly, tightly wrap the loaf in plastic wrap. Then place it in a zip-top freezer bag. The double-wrap is the secret to freshness. It creates a barrier between bread and freezer air to avoid exposing the bread to freezer burn.

4. Date the wrapped loaf and place it in the freezer.

5. Bread will keep for 3 to 6 months, but keep in mind flavors will begin to dull after a month.

When you would like to use the bread, remove it from the freezer, allow it to thaw, wrap foil around the bread and then heat in the oven for 15 minutes at 300 °F.

CHAPTER 5:
TROUBLESHOOTING

So, the time has come to finally open up the bread machine, but low and behold, the bread that you have so hoped for resembles nothing of the sort. Flops and spills do happen from time to time. Here are a few answers to the questions you may have, depending on the appearance of your bread.

MY LOAF WASN'T COOKED INSIDE.

If you bite into your bread and are left feeling like you are chewing on a piece of gum, then your thermostat could be faulty. If this frequently occurs, then look at your machine's thermostat since it's probably the problem.

Using extra sugar or not measuring out your wet ingredients properly can also cause this to happen.

MY LOAF DIDN'T RISE OR ONLY ROSE HALFWAY.

So, your bread looks like a giant fluffed up pancake and nothing like a loaf of bread? Old yeast, or forgotten yeast, will be your biggest culprit.

If too much salt was added, then you might be faced with a flat version of your bread, too, as the yeast won't be able to work properly (salt plays as an inhibitor to the yeast). The same issue might occur due to adding ingredients into the bread machine in the wrong order. Always follow the bread machine's instructions to prevent things like this from happening.

Specific flours also may contribute to this problem. Different flours will give different rises. Bread flour will give you a bigger loaf than all-purpose flour, while rye flour will give you a smaller loaf.

IT LOOKS LIKE A MUSHROOM.

If your bread resembles a cloud that is left behind when a large bomb explodes, then you need to brush up on your measuring techniques. Often this is down to incorrect ingredient measurements.

Secondly, if you know deep down that you measured correctly, and followed the recipe step-by-step, then it could be due to your bread machine's pan size being too small for the job.

MY BREAD IS FAR TOO DENSE.

For starters, dense bread could be down to having added too much or too little of something. It might happen if you add more nuts or dried fruit than needed. Adding more whole-grain flour than needed will also affect the outcome of your bread.

If the recipe calls for only plain bread flour and you would like to incorporate whole-grain flour, consider using half of each rather than swapping out one ingredient entirely.

THERE ARE BIG HOLES IN MY BREAD.

If your bread has holes too big and uneven, I suggest you can cast your gaze upon three culprits: yeast, salt, or water.

Excess yeast can be the cause for extra air bubbles creating holes in the baked loaf.

Or sometimes, if it is too warm in your kitchen, the yeast may have gotten more "oomph" than it needed causing the texture of your bread to change. In this case, and if you choose to make another loaf, use a pinch less yeast in your recipe.

If you skipped the salt, then holes may appear in your bread.

Too much water can do the same for your bread.

Adding nuts, fruits, or vegetables that have been rinsed or preserved in another liquid? Take a cloth and dry them off before adding them in.

MY BREAD IS CAVED-IN.

When opening the bread maker, you could be greeted by what looks like a prize-winning loaf of bread only to watch it cave in on itself. First things first, leave the machine to do its thing. Often, if you open and close the machine regularly while it is baking, this can cause your bread to collapse. The same might happen if you have not added salt or added too much yeast.

It is also very important to know what the capacity of your bread pan is. If your bread pan is too small for the job, then your bread may collapse.

MY BREAD IS UNEVEN.

If your bread is uneven or lopsided, it could be that the bread machine's mixing paddles are not churning evenly or are out of rhythm with each other. Paddles can be worn out over time, so it is worth checking them if you have had your bread machine for some time. Alternatively, one of the paddles may have become wedged during the churning or kneading process.

MY BREAD TASTES OFF.

The bread is perfect, just as you imagined it to be, but when you finally bite into it, it tastes weird or, frankly, just tastes bad. This is down to your ingredients and their freshness. Make sure you are storing your ingredients correctly and using the freshest ingredients possible.

CHAPTER 6:
CLASSIC BREADS

COUNTRY-STYLED WHITE BREAD

Time: 2 hours and 20 minutes / **Prep Time:** 15 minutes / **Cook Time:** 2 hours and 5 minutes

Nutrition Facts per slice:

Calories: 122 kcal / ***Total fat:*** *5 g* / ***Saturated fat:*** *1 g* / ***Cholesterol:*** *0 mg* / ***Total carbohydrates:*** *17 g* / ***Dietary fiber:*** *2 g* ***Sodium:*** *394 mg* / ***Protein:*** *2 g*

Flavor and taste:

Lovely doughy texture, delicious either served fresh or toasted.

Ingredients:

	1 Pound loaf	1 ½ Pound loaf	2 Pound loaf
Lukewarm water	1 ½ cups	2 ¼ cups	3 cups
Extra-virgin olive oil	1 ½ tbsp	2 tbsp	3 tbsp
Plain bread flour	1 cup	1 ½ cups	2 cups
White all-purpose Flour	2 ½ cups	3 ¾ cups	5 cups
Baking soda	¼ tsp	½ tsp	½ tsp
Sugar	1 ½ tsp	2 ½ tsp	3 tsp
Salt	1 pinch	½ tsp	½ tsp
Bread machine yeast	2 ½ tsp	3 tsp	5 tsp

Directions:

1. Add the ingredients into the bread machine as per the order of the ingredients listed above or follow your bread machine's instruction manual.
2. Select the rapid setting and the medium crust function.
3. When ready, turn the bread out onto a drying rack and allow it to cool, then serve.

Tip(s):

1. I made this bread using the rapid cycle on my bread machine. Alternatively, you can make this recipe using the regular setting, adding in only two teaspoons of yeast instead.
2. Check your bread machine when kneading. If the dough appears wet, add in a few teaspoons of flour. If the dough is too dense, add a few teaspoons of water.

HONEY AND MILK WHITE BREAD

Time: 3 hours 10 minutes / **Prep Time:** 10 minutes / **Cook Time:** 3 hours

Nutrition Facts per slice:

Calories: 102.5 kcal / ***Total fat:*** *1.9 g* / ***Saturated fat:*** *0.7 g* / ***Cholesterol:*** *2.4 mg* / ***Total carbohydrates:*** *18.3 g* / ***Dietary fiber:*** *0.7 g* / ***Sodium:*** *202.8 mg* / ***Protein:*** *2.9 g*

Flavor and taste:

A soft, light, and fluffy bread that will find you repeating this recipe weekly, if not more.

Ingredients:

	1 Pound loaf	1 ½ Pound loaf	2 Pound loaf
Lukewarm whole milk	½ cup	1 cup	1 ¼ cups
Unsalted butter	¾ tbsp	1 ¼ tbsp	1 ½ tbsp
Honey	¾ tbsp	1 ¼ tbsp	1 ½ tbsp
White all-purpose Flour	1 ½ cups	2 ¼ cups	3 cups
Salt	1 pinch	1 pinch	1 pinch
Bread machine yeast	2/4 tsp	1 ¼ tsp	1 ½ tsp

Directions:

1. Add the ingredients into the bread machine as per the order of the ingredients listed above or follow your bread machine's instruction manual.
2. Select the white bread function and the light crust function.
3. When ready, turn the bread out onto a drying rack and allow it to cool, then serve.

Tip(s):

1. You are welcome to add another 1 ½ tablespoons of honey to sweeten the bread further as per your taste.

BUTTER BREAD

Time: 3 hours and 45 minutes / **Prep Time:** 10 minutes / **Cook Time:** 3 hours and 35 minutes

Nutrition Facts per slice:

Calories: 262.2 kcal / **Total fat:** 13.5 g / **Saturated fat:** 8.2 g / **Cholesterol:** 58.6 mg / **Total carbohydrates** 29.8 g / **Dietary fiber:** 1.3 g / **Sodium:** 45.3 mg / **Protein:** 5.9 g

Flavor and taste:

A very simple recipe to follow that delivers on taste. It is a soft bread that is perfect for mopping up leftover soups and stews on cold winter nights.

Ingredients:

	1 Pound loaf	1 ½ Pound loaf	2 Pound loaf
Egg	1	1 ½	2
Lukewarm whole milk	1 ¼ cup	1 ¾ cup	2 ½ cup
Unsalted butter, diced	½ cup	¾ cup	1 ⅛ cup
Plain bread flour	2 cups	3 ¼ cup	4 ⅓ cup
Salt	1 pinch	1 ½ pinches	2 pinches
Sugar	1 pinch	1 ½ pinches	2 pinches
Instant dry yeast	2 tsp	3 tsp	4 tsp

Directions:

1. Add the ingredients into the bread machine as per the order of the ingredients listed above or follow your bread machine's instruction manual.
2. Select the French setting and medium crust function.
3. When ready, turn the bread out onto a drying rack and allow it to cool, then serve.

Tip(s):

1. If your bread maker does not have a French setting select the white bread function.

BASIC WHITE BREAD

Time: 3 hours and 10 minutes / **Prep Time:** 10 minutes / **Cook Time:** 3 hours

Nutrition Facts per slice:

Calories: 110 kcal / *Total fat:* 2 g / *Saturated fat:* 1.3 g / *Cholesterol:* 5.5 mg / *Total carbohydrates:* 20.3 g / *Dietary fiber* 0.9 g / *Sodium:* 130.8 mg / *Protein* 2.8 g

Flavor and taste:

Nothing beats a freshly sliced piece of white bread, and this recipe delivers on that promise.

Ingredients:

	1 Pound loaf	1 ½ Pound loaf	2 Pound loaf
Lukewarm water	½ cup	¾ cup	1 cup
Lukewarm whole milk	¼ cup	½ cup	⅓ cup
Unsalted butter, diced	1 ½ tbsp	2 ¼ tbsp	3 tbsp
White all-purpose Flour	1 ¾ cups	2 ¼ cups	3 ¾ cups
Sugar	1 ½ tbsp	2 ¼ tbsp	3 tbsp
Salt	¾ tsp	1 ⅛ tsp	1 ½ tsp
Instant dry yeast	¾ tsp	1 ⅛ tsp	1 ½ tsp

Directions:

1. Add the ingredients into the bread machine as per the order of the ingredients listed above or follow your bread machine's instruction manual.
2. Select the basic loaf setting and the medium crust function.
3. When ready, turn the bread out onto a drying rack and allow it to cool, then serve.

Tip(s):

1. This bread can store for up to four days if kept in a cloth bag, away from sunlight.

50/50 Bread

Time: 3 hours and 55 minutes / **Prep Time:** 10 minutes / **Cook Time:** 3 hours and 45 minutes

Nutrition Facts per slice:

Calories: 106 kcal / *Total fat:* 2 g / *Saturated fat:* 1 g / *Cholesterol:* 4 mg / *Total carbohydrates:* 19 g / *Dietary fiber:* 2 g *Sodium:* 235 mg / *Protein:* 3 g

Flavor and taste:

I love this combination. This recipe provides you with a much lighter textured bread than a 100% whole wheat bread.

Ingredients:

	1 Pound loaf	**1 ½ Pound loaf**	**2 Pound loaf**
Lukewarm water	½ cup	¾ cup	1 cup
Honey	½ tbsp	¾ tbsp	1 tbsp
Unsalted butter, diced	1 tbsp	1 ½ tbsp	2 tbsp
Plain bread flour	¾ cup	1 ⅛ cups	1 ½ cups
Whole wheat flour	¾ cup	1 ⅛ cups	1 ½ cups
Brown sugar	¾ tbsp	1 ⅛ tbsp	1 ½ tbsp
Powdered milk	¾ tbsp	1 ⅛ tbsp	1 ½ tbsp
Salt	¾ tsp	1 ⅛ tsp	1 ⅓ tsp
Instant dry yeast	½ tsp	¾ tsp	1 tsp

Directions:

1. Add the ingredients into the bread machine as per the order of the ingredients listed above or follow your bread machine's instruction manual.
2. Select the whole-wheat setting and medium crust function.
3. When ready, turn the bread out onto a drying rack and allow it to cool, then serve.

Tip(s):

1. For a less toasted crust, choose the light function on your bread machine.
2. Sprinkle some sesame seeds on top for more flavor.

CLASSIC FRENCH BREAD

Time: 3 hours and 15 minutes / **Prep Time:** 15 minutes / **Cook Time:** 3 hours

Nutrition Facts per slice:

Calories: 206 kcal / *Total fat:* 0.6 g / *Saturated fat:* 0.1 g / *Cholesterol:* 0 mg *Total carbohydrates:* 43.4 g / *Dietary fiber:* 1.8 g *Sodium:* 292.2 mg / *Protein:* 5.9 g

Flavor and taste:

A great combination of crunchy and chewy textures.

Ingredients:

	1 Pound loaf	1 ½ Pound loaf	2 Pound loaf
Lukewarm water	1 cup	1 ¼ cups	1 ¼ cups
Sugar	2 tsp	1 tbsp	1 tbsp
Salt	1 tsp	1 ½ tsp	1 ½ tsp
Plain bread flour	3 ¼ cups	3 ⅔ cups	4 cups
Bread machine yeast	1 tsp	1 ½ tsp	1 ½ tsp

Directions:

1. Add the ingredients into the bread machine as per the order of the ingredients listed above or follow your bread machine's instruction manual.
2. Select the French setting and medium crust function.
3. When ready, turn the bread out onto a drying rack and allow it to cool, then serve.

Tip(s):

1. To flavor the bread, add in half a cup of dried cranberries or raisins for a sweeter flavor. For a savory flavor, add in the leaves from two sprigs of rosemary.

SOURDOUGH

Time: 3 hours and 20 minutes / **Prep Time:** 20 minutes for bread, 5 days for sourdough starter / **Cook Time:** 3 hours

Nutrition Facts per slice:

Calories: 181.3 kcal / *Total fat:* 4.5 g / *Saturated fat:* 0.6 g
Cholesterol: 0 mg / *Total carbohydrates:* 30.4 g / *Dietary fiber:* 1.3 g / *Sodium:* 467 mg / Protein: 4.4 g

Flavor and taste:

A rich, chewy textured bread that carries a hint of tang due to the sourdough starter.

Ingredients for a sourdough starter:

- 2 cups white, all-purpose flour
- 1 tsp active dry yeast
- 2 cups lukewarm water

Ingredients for bread:

	1 Pound loaf	1 ½ Pound loaf	2 Pound loaf
Sourdough starter	½ cup	¾ cup	1 cup
Lukewarm water	⅓ cup	½ cup	¾ cup
Sugar	½ tbsp	¾ tbsp	1 tbsp
Active dry yeast	½ tbsp	¾ tbsp	1 tbsp
Plain bread flour	1 ½ cups	2 ¼ cups	3 cups
Vegetable oil	1 ½ tbsp	2 ¼ tbsp	3 tbsp
Salt	1 tsp	1 ½ tsp	2 tsp

Directions for a sourdough starter:

1. Combine the ingredients in a glass or ceramic dish. Ensure the dish is big enough to allow for expansion.
2. Cover the dish with cloth, fix the cloth into place using an elastic band.
3. Allow the starter to rest for five days in a warm area. Stir the starter once a day.
4. Your starter sourdough is now ready for use. Refrigerate the remainder and use it when needed. If you would like to make a few loaves, you can keep the sourdough starter *"alive"* by feeding it equal amounts of flour and water and allowing it to rest in a warm area and using it when needed.

Directions for bread:

1. Add the sourdough starter, water, sugar, and yeast into the bread maker. Using a spatula, combine the ingredients.
2. Allow it to rest for ten minutes.
3. Add bread flour, oil, and salt.
4. Select the basic setting and medium crust function.
5. When ready, turn the bread out onto a drying rack and allow it to cool, then serve.

CHAPTER 7: WHOLE-WHEAT BREADS

WHOLE WHEAT BREAD

Time: 3 hours and 15 minutes / **Prep Time:** 15 minutes / **Cook Time:** 3 hours

Nutrition Facts per slice:

Calories: 131.6 *kcal* / *Total fat:* 3.2 g / *Saturated fat:* 1.8 g / *Cholesterol:* 8 mg / *Total carbohydrates:* 22.9 g / *Dietary fiber:* 2.1 g / *Sodium:* 139.3 mg / *Protein:* 3.9 g

Flavor and taste:

This is a filling, wholesome bread that my whole family enjoys. I always sprinkle extra oats, seeds, or multigrain into it to give it more of a rustic look and taste.

Ingredients:

	1 Pound loaf	**1 ½ Pound loaf**	**2 Pound loaf**
Lukewarm whole milk	½ cup	1 cup	1 ⅓ cups
Unsalted butter, diced	2 tbsp	3 tbsp	4 tbsp
Whole wheat flour	1 cup	1 ½ cups	2 cups
Plain bread flour	1 cup	1 ½ cups	2 cups
Brown sugar	2 ½ tbsp	3 ¾ tbsp	5 tbsp
Salt	¾ tsp	1 ¼ tsp	1 ½ tsp
Bread machine yeast	¾ tsp	1 ¼ tsp	1 ½ tsp

Directions:
1. Add the ingredients into the bread machine as per the order of the ingredients listed above or follow your bread machine's instruction manual.
2. Select the whole wheat setting and medium crust function.
3. When ready, turn the bread out onto a drying rack and allow it to cool, then serve.

Tip(s):
1. After the bread has kneaded for the first time, sprinkle oats or seeds over the top and then allow the machine to continue baking.

WHOLE WHEAT AND HONEY BREAD

Time: 3 hours and 10 minutes / **Prep Time:** 10 minutes / **Cook Time:** 3 hours

Nutrition Facts per slice:

Calories: *180 kcal* / ***Total fat:*** *3.5 g* / ***Saturated fat:*** *0 g* / ***Cholesterol:*** *0 mg* / ***Total carbohydrates:*** *33.4 g* / ***Dietary fiber:*** *2.8 g* / ***Sodium:*** *79 mg* / ***Protein:*** *5.2 g*

Flavor and taste:

A bread, full of flavor, and super tasty, perfect with a smear of butter and honey.

Ingredients:

	1 Pound loaf	**1 ½ Pound loaf**	**2 Pound loaf**
Lukewarm water	1 ⅛ cups	1 ½ cups	2 ¼ cups
Honey	3 tbsp	4 ½ tbsp	6 tbsp
Vegetable oil	2 tbsp	3 tbsp	4 tbsp
Plain bread flour	1 ½ cups	2 ¼ cups	3 cups
Whole wheat flour	1 ½ cups	2 ¼ cups	3 cups
Salt	⅓ tsp	¼ tsp	½ tsp
Instant dry yeast	1 ½ tsp	2 ¼ tsp	3 tsp

Directions:

1. Add the ingredients into the bread machine as per the order of the ingredients listed above or follow your bread machine's instruction manual.
2. Select the whole wheat setting and medium crust function.
3. When ready, turn the bread out onto a drying rack and allow it to cool, then serve.

Tip(s):

1. When the bread is ready, glaze the top with honey and add a few sesame seeds or rolled oats.

Whole Wheat Seeds and Syrup Bread

Time: 3 hours and 5 minutes / **Prep Time:** 5 minutes / **Cook Time:** 3 hours

Nutritional facts per slice:

Calories: 120 kcal / *Total fat:* 5 g / *Saturated fat:* 0 g / *Cholesterol:* 0 mg / *Total carbohydrates:* 21 g / *Dietary fiber:* 3 g / *Sodium:* 200 mg / *Protein:* 4 g

Flavor and taste:

Solid, yet slightly sweet, this bread is a great choice for daily sandwiches and toasted snacks.

Ingredients:

	1 Pound Loaf	1 ½ Pound Loaf	2 Pound Loaf
Lukewarm water	⅔ cup	1 cup	1 ¼ cups
Olive oil	1 tbsp	1 ½ tbsp	2 tbsp
Maple syrup	2 tbsp	2 ½ tbsp	¼ cup
White whole wheat flour	1 ¾ cups	2 ⅔ cups	3 ½ cups
Assorted seeds (an even mix of flax, sesame and/or sunflower seeds)	6 tsp	8 tsp	¼ cup
Salt	¾ tsp	1 tsp	1 ½ tsp
Instant yeast	¾ tsp	1 tsp	1 ½ tsp

Directions:
1. Place all ingredients into your bread machine in the exact order listed.
2. Select the whole-wheat setting and the medium crust function.
3. When ready, turn the bread out onto a drying rack so it can cool, then serve.

Tip(s):
1. Remember: after your bread machine has kneaded the dough for 10 minutes, quickly examine its consistency. If all is well, your dough should be smooth. If it feels sticky, add some flour. If it feels chunky, add some more water. After that, you should be all set.
2. If you wish for enhanced texture, add one egg for every cup of flour. This should be done after the seeds, but before the salt.
3. To shake things up, you can replace the seeds with muesli.

100% Whole Wheat Bread

Time: 4 hours and 5 minutes / **Prep Time:** 5 minutes / **Cook Time:** 4 hours

Nutrition Facts per slice:

Calories: 147.9 kcal / *Total fat:* 1 g / *Saturated fat:* 0.5 g / *Cholesterol:* 1.9 mg / *Total carbohydrates:* 30.4 g / *Dietary fiber:* 0.9 g / *Sodium:* 206.7 mg / *Protein:* 4.0 g

Flavor and taste:

A wonderful whole wheat bread that rises well, it has just the right amount of density and lightness.

Ingredients:

	1 Pound loaf	**1 ½ Pound loaf**	**2 Pound loaf**
Lukewarm water	1 cup	1 ½ cups	2 cups
Milk powder	1 ¼ tbsp	2 tbsp	2 ½ tbsp
Unsalted butter, diced	1 ¼ tbsp	2 tbsp	2 ½ tbsp
Honey	1 ¼ tbsp	2 tbsp	2 ⅓ tbsp
Molasses	1 ¼ tbsp	2 tbsp	2 ½ tbsp
Salt	1 tsp	1 ½ tsp	2 tsp
Whole wheat flour	2 ¼ cups	3 ⅓ cups	4 ½ cups
Active dry yeast	1 tsp	1 ½ tsp	2 tsp

Directions:

1. Add the ingredients into the bread machine as per the order of the ingredients listed above or follow your bread machine's instruction manual.
2. Select the whole wheat setting and medium crust function.
3. When ready, turn the bread out onto a drying rack and allow it to cool, then serve.

Tip(s):

1. I combine the milk powder and water before adding them to the bread machine.

Seeded Whole Wheat Bread

Time: 3 hours and 10 minutes / **Prep Time:** 10 minutes / **Cook Time:** 3 hours

Nutrition Facts per slice:

Calories: 84 kcal / *Total fat:* 2 g / *Saturated fat:* 1 g / *Cholesterol:* 2 mg / *Total carbohydrates:* 14 g / *Dietary fiber:* 1 g *Sodium:* 133 mg / *Protein:* 3 g

Flavor and taste:

A delightful, crunchy whole wheat bread that is full of flavor thanks to the added seeds.

Ingredients:

	1 Pound loaf	1 ½ Pound loaf	2 Pound loaf
Lukewarm water	⅔ cups	1 cup	1 ¼ cups
Milk powder	3 tbsp	4 ½ tbsp	6 tbsp
Honey	1 tbsp	1 ½ tbsp	2 tbsp
Unsalted butter, softened	1 tbsp	1 ½ tbsp	2 tbsp
Plain bread flour	1 cup	1 ½ cups	2 cups
Whole wheat flour	1 cup	1 ½ cups	2 cups
Poppy seeds	2 tbsp	3 tbsp	4 tbsp
Sesame seeds	2 tbsp	3 tbsp	4 tbsp
Sunflower seeds	2 tbsp	3 tbsp	4 tbsp
Salt	¾ tsp	1 ⅛ tsp	1 ½ tsp
Instant dry yeast	2 tsp	3 tsp	4 tsp

Directions:

1. Add the ingredients into the bread machine as per the order of the ingredients listed above or follow your bread machine's instruction manual.
2. Select the basic setting and medium crust function.
3. When ready, turn the bread out onto a drying rack and allow it to cool, then serve.

Tip(s):

1. Feel free to make use of any fine seeds, such as pumpkin or sesame seeds.

Honey and Oatmeal Whole Wheat Bread

Time: 3 hours and 10 minutes / **Prep Time:** 10 minutes / **Cook Time:** 3 hours

Nutritional facts per slice:

Calories: 173.1 kcal / *Total fat:* 2.1 g / *Saturated fat:* 0.3 g / *Cholesterol:* 0 mg / *Total carbohydrates:* 35.2 g / *Dietary fiber:* 2.8 g / *Sodium:* 196.1 mg / *Protein:* 4.7 g

Flavor and taste:

A healthy bread that manages to be soft and sweet without any raw sugar added. Great if you want to combine the sweetness of the honey recipe with the rustic flavor of rolled oats!

Ingredients:

	1 Pound Loaf	1 ½ Pound Loaf	2 Pound Loaf
Lukewarm water	⅔ cup	1 cup	1 ¼ cups
Olive oil	½ tbsp	2 ¼ tsp	1 tbsp
Honey	8 tsp	¼ cup	⅓ cup
Rolled oats	½ cup	½ cup and 4 tbsp	1 cup
Whole wheat flour	¾ cup	1 cup and 2 tbsp	1 ½ cups
White bread flour	¾ cup	1 cup and 2 tbsp	1 ½ cups
Salt	½ tsp	¾ tsp	1 tsp
Instant yeast	½ tsp	¾ tsp	1 tsp

Directions:
1. All ingredients should enter your bread machine either in the order listed or according to your bread machine's instruction manual.
2. Select the basic bread setting and soft crust function.
3. When ready, turn the bread out onto a drying rack so it can cool, then serve.

Tip(s):
1. Feel free to add raisins to sweeten the loaf further.
2. Yeast amount can be doubled to enhance the rise.
3. Oat bran can be used in place of rolled oats.
4. For a 2-pound loaf, having 2 cups of whole wheat flour to one cup of white bread flour can increase the overall density without going overboard.

CHAPTER 8:

CHEESE & ITALIAN STYLED BREADS

CLOSE-GRAINED CHEDDAR CHEESE BREAD

Time: 3 hours and 40 minutes / **Prep Time:** 5 minutes / **Cook Time:** 3 hours 35 minutes

Nutritional facts per slice:

Calories: 150 kcal / *Total fat:* 3.5 g / *Saturated fat:* 2 g / *Cholesterol:* 10 mg
Total carbohydrates: 19 g / *Dietary fiber:* 1 g / *Sodium:* 320 mg / *Protein:* 5 g

Flavor and taste:

If you love cheddar, you'll love this bread. This savory loaf is great when you want to add an extra tang to your sandwiches, or when you wish to enhance the flavor balance of any other cheeses you place on top. It goes very well with hot tomato soups, as well as grilled-cheese sandwiches.

Ingredients:

	1 Pound Loaf	1 ½ Pound Loaf	2 Pound Loaf
Lukewarm milk	½ cup	½ cup and 4 tbsp	1 cup
Plain bread flour	1 ½ cups	2 ¼ cups	3 cups
Salt	⅔ tsp	1 tsp	1 ¼ tsp
Sugar	½ tbsp	2 ½ tsp	1 tbsp
Extra-sharp cheddar, grated	½ cup	⅔ cup	1 cup
Parmesan cheese, grated	6 tsp	8 tsp	¼ cup
Instant yeast	¾ tsp	1 tsp	1 ½ tsp

Directions:

1. Place all ingredients into your bread machine in the exact order listed.
2. Select the basic cycle setting and the soft crust function.
3. When ready, turn the bread out onto a drying rack so it can cool, then serve.

Tip(s):

1. After your bread machine has kneaded the dough for 10 minutes, quickly examine its consistency. If all is well, your dough should be mostly smooth, but slightly sticky. Add flour if it's too sticky, or milk if it's too chunky.
2. If you wish to add a little extra bite to your bread, you can literally spice things up by adding between ½ to 1 tsp of tabasco sauce. This should be added last, after the yeast, but before you begin kneading.
3. This bread goes especially well with rosemary. Feel free to season your fresh loaf with some while it is cooling down, or add it later as part of a sandwich.

OLIVE BREAD

Time: 2 hours and 10 minutes / **Prep Time:** 10 minutes / **Cook Time:** 2 hours

Nutrition Facts per slice:

*Calories: 172 kcal / **Total fat:** 19.1 g / **Saturated fat:** 2.6 g / Cholesterol: 0 mg / **Total carbohydrates:** 215.6 g / **Dietary fiber:** 11 g / **Sodium:** 2149.8 mg / **Protein:** 30.2 g*

Flavor and taste:

It is a fragrant bread that can be served with a smear of butter or with pates and Italian deli meats.

Ingredients:

	1 Pound loaf	**1 ½ Pound loaf**	**2 Pound loaf**
Lukewarm water	½ cup	1 cup	1 ¼ cup
Extra-virgin olive oil	½ tbsp	1 tbsp	1 ¼ tbsp
Plain bread flour	2 cups	3 cups	4 cups
Salt	1 pinch	1 pinch	1 ½ pinches
Sugar	1 ¼ tbsp	2 tbsp	2 ½ tbsp
Bread machine yeast	¾ tbsp	1 ¼ tbsp	1 ½ tbsp
Pitted black olives, finely diced	½ cup	¾ cup	1 cup

Directions:

1. Add the ingredients into the bread machine as per the order of the ingredients listed above or follow your bread machine's instruction manual. Do not add the olives in yet.
2. Select the basic setting or wheat function, and the medium crust function.
3. Add the diced olives when the machine signals that mix-in ingredients may be included. If your machine does not have this functionality, add the olives after the first kneading cycle.
4. When ready, turn the bread out onto a drying rack and allow it to cool, then serve.

Tip(s):

1. If your olives are in brine, be sure to pat them dry before dicing them and adding them into your bread mixture.

GARLIC AND HERB BREAD

Time: 2 hours and 10 minutes / **Prep Time:** 10 minutes / **Cook Time:** 2 hours

Nutrition Facts per slice:

Calories: 203.8 kcal / *Total fat:* 2.2 g / *Saturated fat:* 1.2 g / *Cholesterol:* 5.4 mg / *Total carbohydrates:* 39 g / *Dietary fiber:* 1.5 g / *Sodium:* 451.4 mg / *Protein:* 6.2 g

Flavor and taste:

Garlicky and delicious. All the right flavors in one mouth-watering bread. Serve the bread with a mild cheese or with a bowl of hearty, vegetable soup.

Ingredients:

	1 Pound loaf	1 ½ Pound loaf	2 Pound loaf
Unsalted butter, diced	1 tbsp	1 ½ tbsp	2 tbsp
Lukewarm 1% milk	1 cup	1 ½ cups	2 cups
White all-purpose flour	3 cups	2 ¼ cup	6 cups
Italian seasoning	1 ½ tsp	2 ¼ tsp	3 tsp
Garlic powder	3 tsp	4 ½ tsp	6 tsp
Sugar	1 tbsp	1 ½ tbsp	2 tbsp
Salt	1 ½ tsp	2 ¼ tsp	3 tsp
Instant dry yeast	2 tsp	3 tsp	4 tsp

Directions:

1. Add the ingredients into the bread machine as per the order of the ingredients listed above or follow your bread machine's instruction manual.
2. Select the basic setting and medium crust function.
3. When ready, turn the bread out onto a drying rack and allow it to cool, then serve.

Tip(s):

1. If you are not a big lover of garlic, you may add two teaspoons of garlic powder to the recipe instead.

ITALIAN PARMESAN BREAD

Time: 3 hours and 10 minutes / **Prep Time:** 10 minutes / **Cook Time:** 3 hours

Nutrition Facts per slice:

Calories: 103.1 kcal / *Total fat:* 0.4 g / *Saturated fat:* 0.1 g / *Cholesterol:* 0.2 mg / *Total carbohydrates:* 21.3 g / *Dietary fiber:* 0.8 g / *Sodium:* 14.1 g / *Protein:* 3 g

Flavor and taste:

The bread has an aromatic taste that is full of Mediterranean flavor.

Ingredients:

	1 Pound loaf	**1 ½ Pound loaf**	**2 Pound loaf**
Lukewarm water	¾ cups	1 ¼ cups	1 ½ cups
White all-purpose flour	2 cups	3 cups	4 cups
Shredded parmesan cheese	⅛ cup	¼ cup	¼ cup
Salt	¾ tsp	1 ⅛ tsp	1 ½ tsp
Italian mixed herbs	½ tsp	¾ tsp	1 tsp
Garlic powder	½ tsp	¾ tsp	1 tsp
Instant dry yeast	1 ¼ tsp	1 ¾ tsp	2 ½ tsp

Directions:

1. Add the ingredients into the bread machine as per the order of the ingredients listed above or follow your bread machine's instruction manual.
2. Select the basic setting and medium crust function.
3. When ready, turn the bread out onto a drying rack and allow it to cool, then serve.

Tip(s):

1. Finely diced fresh herbs work just as well in place of the dried herbs.

Pepperoni and Cheese Bread

Time: 3 hours and 10 minutes / **Prep Time:** 10 minutes / **Cook Time:** 3 hours

Nutritional facts per slice:

Calories: 95.02 *kcal* / *Total fat:* 0.71 *g* / *Saturated fat:* 0.47 *g* / *Cholesterol:* 1.64 *mg* / *Total carbohydrates:* 18.85 *g* / *Dietary fiber:* 0.72 *g* / *Sodium:* 13.92 *mg* / *Protein:* 2.93 *g*

Flavor and taste:

A bread that is soft and fluffy on the inside, while nice and crusty on the outside. Gives a delicious, spicy hint of oregano and pepperoni without being overwhelming.

Ingredients:

	1 Pound Loaf	1 ½ Pound Loaf	2 Pound Loaf
Lukewarm water	½ cup and 1 tbsp	¾ cup	1 cup and 2 tbsp
Mozzarella cheese	4 tbsp	¼ cup	⅓ cup
Sugar	1 tbsp	1 ½ tbsp	2 tbsp
Garlic salt	¾ tsp	1 tsp	1 ½ tsp
Dried oregano	¾ tsp	1 tsp	1 ½ tsp
All-purpose flour	1 ⅔ cup	2 ⅓ cups	3 ¼ cups
Active dry yeast	¾ tsp	1 tsp	1 ½ tsp
Diced pepperoni	⅓ cup	½ cup	⅔ cup

Directions:

1. Add all ingredients, except the pepperoni, to the bread machine, either in the order listed, or according to your bread machine's instruction manual.
2. Select the basic bread setting and the medium crust function.
3. Just before your bread machine enters its final kneading cycle (most machines will signal you with a beep around this time), add the pepperoni.
4. When ready, turn the bread out onto a drying rack so it can cool, then serve.

Tip(s):

1. This recipe <u>does not</u> work well with the delay timer feature.
2. Adding an extra ½ or 1 tbsp of vegetable oil can lift the flavor, if necessary.
3. Cheese amounts can be tripled to increase the flavor.
4. Oregano can be substituted with any Italian seasoning.

QUICK BAKE ITALIAN BREAD

Time: 1 hour and 45 minutes / **Prep Time:** 14 minutes / **Cook Time:** 1 hour and 20 minutes

Nutrition Facts per slice:

Calories: 126 *kcal* / ***Total fat:*** *3 g* / ***Saturated fat:*** *1 g* / ***Cholesterol:*** *6 mg* / ***Total carbohydrates:*** *22 g* / ***Dietary fiber:*** *1 g* / ***Sodium:*** *109 mg* / ***Protein:*** *4 g*

Flavor and taste:

Viva Italiano, the most delectable Italian bread you will ever make. It is soft and fragrant, and extra yummy served with a winter soup.

Ingredients:

	1 Pound loaf	1 ½ Pound loaf	2 Pound loaf
Lukewarm water	¾ cup	1 cup	1 ⅔ cups
Unsalted butter, softened	1 tbsp	1 ½ tbsp	2 tbsp
Plain bread flour	2 cups	3 cups	4 ¼ cups
Powdered milk	1 ½ tbsp	2 ¼ tbsp	3 tbsp
Dried marjoram	¾ tsp	1 ¼ tsp	1 ½ tsp
Dried basil	¾ tsp	1 ¼ tsp	1 ½ tsp
Dried thyme	½ tsp	¾ tsp	1 tsp
Salt	¼ tsp	1 pinch	⅔ tsp
Sugar	1 ½ tbsp	2 ¼ tbsp	3 tbsp
Instant dry yeast	2 tsp	3 tsp	4 tsp

Directions:

1. Add the ingredients into the bread machine as per the order of the ingredients listed above or follow your bread machine's instruction manual.
2. Select the quick or rapid setting and medium crust function.
3. When ready, turn the bread out onto a drying rack and allow it to cool, then serve.

Tip(s):

1. Ensure that your olives have been patted dry before using them in this recipe as olive brine affects the yeast.

CIABATTA

Time: 2 hours and 40 minutes / **Prep Time:** 2 hours and 10 minutes / **Cook Time:** 30 minutes

Nutrition Facts per slice:

Calories: 190 kcal / *Total fat:* 2.2 g / *Saturated fat:* 0.3 g / *Cholesterol:* 0 mg / *Total carbohydrates:* 36.6 g / *Dietary fiber:* 1.4 g / *Sodium:* 441 mg / *Protein:* 5.1 g

Flavor and taste:

An authentic Mediterranean bread with a crispy crust. Ideal when served with a swirl of extra virgin olive oil and balsamic vinegar.

Tip(s):

1. This is a sticky dough, so do not add extra flour though you may feel the need to do so.

Ingredients:

	1 Pound loaf	1 ½ Pound loaf	2 Pound loaf
Lukewarm water	¾ cup	1 ⅛ cup	1 ½ cups
Extra-virgin olive oil	½ tbsp	¾ tbsp	1 tbsp
All-purpose flour	1 ½ cups	2 ¼ cup	3 ¼ cup
Salt	¾ tsp	1 ⅛ tsp	1 ½ tsp
Sugar	½ tsp	¾ tsp	1 tsp
Bread machine yeast	¾ tsp	1 ⅛ tsp	1 ½ tsp

Directions:

1. Add the ingredients into the bread machine as per the order of the ingredients listed above or follow your bread machine's instruction manual.
2. Select the dough cycle.
3. When the dough is ready, place it onto a floured surface. Cover the dough with a ceramic or glass dish and allow it to rest for ten minutes.
4. Shape the dough an oval shape. Split into two oval shapes when doubling up on the recipe.
5. Place onto a greased baking tray, cover with a cloth and allow to rest for a further 30 minutes or until it has doubled in size. Allow the dough to rest in a dry, warm area of your kitchen.
6. Preheat your oven to 425 °F.
7. Using the bottom end of a wooden spoon make small indents on the top of each loaf. Drive the spoon down into the dough until it touches the baking tray. Then place into the oven and bake for 30 minutes.
8. Sprinkle water lightly over the top of the loaves every 10 minutes while baking.
9. When ready, turn the bread out onto a drying rack and allow it to cool, then serve.

BACON AND CHEESE BREAD

Time: 3 hours and 10 minutes / **Prep Time:** 10 minutes / **Cook Time:** 3 hours

Nutrition Facts per slice:

Calories: 171.3 kcal / *Total fat:* 4.6 g / *Saturated fat:* 2.5 g / *Cholesterol:* 26.9 mg / *Total carbohydrates:* 25.8 g / *Dietary fiber:* 1 g / *Sodium:* 283.1 mg / *Protein:* 6.2 g

Flavor and taste:

A rich, savory flavored bread that is delicious served as is or toasted and topped with eggs and bacon the following day.

Ingredients:

	1 Pound loaf	1 ½ Pound loaf	2 Pound loaf
Egg, lightly beaten	½	1	1 ⅓
Lukewarm water	½ cup	1 cup	1 ⅓ cup
Unsalted butter, diced	½ tbsp	1 tbsp	1 ⅓ cup
Shredded cheddar cheese	½ cup	¾ cup	1 cup
Bacon bits	2 tbsp	3 tbsp	4 tbsp
Plain bread flour	2 cups	3 cups	4 cups
Salt	½ tsp	1 tsp	1 ⅓ tsp
Sugar	1 tbsp	1 ½ tbsp	2 tbsp
Active dry yeast	1 tsp	1 ½ tsp	2 tsp

Directions:

1. Add the ingredients into the bread machine as per the order of the ingredients listed above or follow your bread machine's instruction manual.
2. Select the basic cycle and light crust function.
3. When ready, turn the bread out onto a drying rack and allow it to cool, then serve.

Tip(s):

1. Feel free to use other varieties of cheese or make a mixture for added flavor. You may also swap the bacon bits with real, pan crisped bacon bits instead.

SPICED JALAPENO CHEESE BREAD

Time: 3 hours and 10 minutes / **Prep Time:** 10 minutes / **Cook Time:** 3 hours

Nutrition Facts per slice:

Calories: 135 kcal / *Total fat:* 4.9 g / *Saturated fat:* 3 g / *Cholesterol:* 14 mg / *Total carbohydrates:* 18.1 g / *Dietary fiber:* 0.7 g / *Sodium:* 327 mg / *Protein:* 4.6 g

Flavor and taste:

This bread is fragrant with a hint of smokiness and cheesiness, which makes it delectable.

Ingredients:

	1 Pound loaf	1 ½ Pound loaf	2 Pound loaf
Lukewarm water	½ cup	1 cup	1 ¼ cups
Milk powder	2 tbsp	3 tbsp	4 tbsp
Unsalted butter	2 tbsp	3 tbsp	4 tbsp
Plain bread flour	1 ½ cup	2 ¼ cups	3 cups
Cheddar cheese	½ cup	¾ cup	1 cup
Jalapeno pepper, finely diced	½	¾	1
Granulated brown sugar	1 tbsp	1 ½ tbsp	2 tbsp
Salt	1 tsp	1 ½ tsp	2 tsp
Bread machine yeast	¾ tsp	1 ⅛ tsp	1 ½ tsp

Directions:

1. Combine the water and instant milk powder first, then add it to your bread machine.
2. Add the remaining ingredients into the bread machine as per the order of the ingredients listed above or follow your bread machine's instruction manual.
3. Select the basic setting and soft crust function.
4. When ready, turn the bread out onto a drying rack and allow it to cool, then serve.

Tip(s):

1. I removed the seeds from the jalapeno pepper before using it in this recipe. If you like spicy foods, you may add more peppers or leave the seeds in, depending on your taste.

CHAPTER 9:
NUT & SEED BREADS
RYE BREAD WITH CARAWAY

Time: 4 hours and 5 minutes / **Prep Time:** 5 minutes / **Cook Time:** 4 hours

Nutrition Facts per slice:

Calories: 93 kcal / *Total fat:* 2.3 g / *Saturated fat:* 1.3 g / *Cholesterol:* 5 mg / *Total carbohydrates:* 16.5 g / *Dietary fiber:* 2.3 g / *Sodium:* 218 mg / *Protein:* 2.4 g

Flavor and taste:

This bread is a lighter version of your traditional rye bread. The molasses allows just enough sweetness to come through, and the bread is deliciously moist.

Ingredients:

	1 Pound loaf	**1 ½ Pound loaf**	**2 Pound loaf**
Lukewarm water	¾ cup	1 ¼ cups	1 ¾ cups
Unsalted butter, diced	1 tbsp	2 tbsp	3 tbsp
Molasses	1 tbsp	1 tbsp	2 tbsp
Rye flour	½ cup	¾ cup	1 cup
Plain bread flour	1 cup	1 ½ cup	2 ¼ cup
Whole wheat flour	½ cup	¾ cup	1 cup
Milk powder	1 tbsp	2 tbsp	3 tbsp
Salt	¾ tsp	1 tsp	1 ½ tsp
Brown sugar	2 tbsp	3 tbsp	¼ cup
Caraway seeds	1 tbsp	1 tbsp	2 tbsp
Instant dry yeast	1 ¼ tsp	1 ¾ tsp	2 ½ tsp

Directions:

1. Add the ingredients into the bread machine as per the order of the ingredients listed above or follow your bread machine's instruction manual.
2. Select the whole wheat setting and medium crust function.
3. When ready, turn the bread out onto a drying rack and allow it to cool, then serve.

Tip(s):

1. The sweetener can be substituted for the sugar, and the butter can be replaced with extra-virgin olive oil.

Sunflower and Flax Seed Bread

Time: 3 hours and 10 minutes / **Prep Time:** 10 minutes / **Cook Time:** 3 hours

Nutritional facts per slice:

Calories: 140.3 kcal / *Total fat:* 4.2 g / *Saturated fat:* 1.2 g / *Cholesterol:* 4.1 mg / *Total carbohydrates:* 22.7 g / *Dietary fiber:* 3.1 g / *Sodium:* 168.6 mg / *Protein:* 4.2 g

Flavor and taste:

A fine seed bread with a hint of sweetness. It perfectly marries the wholesomeness of whole wheat and the texture of seeds.

Ingredients:

	1 Pound Loaf	**1 ½ Pound Loaf**	**2 Pound Loaf**
Lukewarm water	⅔ cup	1 cup	1 ⅓ cup
Butter, softened	1 tbsp	1 ½ tbsp	2 tbsp
Honey	1 ½ tbsp	2 tbsp and 1 tsp	3 tbsp
Bread flour	¾ cup	1 cup	1 ½ cup
Whole wheat flour	⅔ cup	1 cup	1 ⅓ cup
Salt	½ tsp	¾ tsp	1 tsp
Active dry yeast	½ tsp	¾ tsp	1 tsp
Flax seeds	¼ cup	⅓ cup and 1 tbsp	½ cup
Sunflower seeds	¼ cup	⅓ cup and 1 tbsp	½ cup

Directions:

1. Place all ingredients (except the sunflower seeds) into the bread machine, either in the order listed, or according to your bread machine's instruction manual.
2. Select the basic bread setting, as well as the soft or medium crust function.
3. Just before your bread machine enters its final kneading cycle (most machines will signal you with a beep around this time), add the sunflower seeds.
4. When ready, turn the bread out onto a drying rack so it can cool, then serve.

Tip(s):

1. Flax needs to be finely ground before it is good for you; that's why we add it in at the beginning, and hold only the sunflowers back for the final kneading cycle.
2. Salt can be doubled for a stronger flavor.

Sweet Mixed Nut Bread

Time: 3 hours and 10 minutes / **Prep Time:** 10 minutes / **Cook Time:** 3 hours

Nutritional facts per slice:

Calories: 187 kcal / *Total fat:* 7 g / *Saturated fat:* 1 g / *Cholesterol:* 0 mg / *Total carbohydrates:* 28 g / *Dietary fiber:* 2 g / *Sodium:* 296 mg / *Protein:* 5 g

Flavor and taste:

This bread is subtly sweet with just the right amount of nuts! It carries some of the wholesomeness of whole wheat bread, yet still makes for a lovely, filling snack during cases of the midday chow-downs.

Ingredients:

	1 Pound Loaf	1 ½ Pound Loaf	2 Pound Loaf
Lukewarm water	⅔ cup	1 cup	1 ⅓ cups
Olive oil	1 ⅓ tbsp	2 tbsp	2 ⅔ tbsp
Honey	1 ⅓ tbsp	2 tbsp	2 ⅔ tbsp
Molasses	1 ⅓ tbsp	2 tbsp	2 ⅔ tbsp
Salt	1 tsp	1 ½ tsp	2 tsp
Whole wheat flour	⅔ cup	1 cup	1 ⅓ cups
Plain bread flour	1 ⅓ cups	2 cups	2 ⅔ cups
Active dry yeast	1 ½ tsp	2 ¼ tsp	3 tsp
Pecan nuts	¼ cup	⅓ cup	½ cup
Walnuts	¼ cup	⅓ cup	½ cup

Directions:

1. Place all ingredients (except the pecans and walnuts) into your bread machine, either in the order listed, or according to the instruction manual that came with your bread machine.
2. Select the basic cycle setting and choose the soft crust function.
3. Before the final kneading cycle, add in your pecans and walnuts.
4. When ready, turn the bread out onto a drying rack so it can cool, then serve.

Tip(s):

1. Although it's always wise to check your dough within the first 10-15 minutes of a bread cycle, for this recipe it is recommended that you check your dough 5 minutes after mixing commences. As usual, add 1 tbsp of water if too chunky, or 1 tbsp of flour if too sticky.

Multigrain Sandwich Loaf

Time: 3 hours and 10 minutes / **Prep Time:** 10 minutes / **Cook Time:** 3 hours

Nutrition Facts per slice:

Calories: 194 kcal / ***Total fat:*** 4.8 g / ***Saturated fat:*** 2.7 g / ***Cholesterol:*** 12 mg / ***Total carbohydrates:*** 33.1 g / ***Dietary fiber:*** 1.4 g / ***Sodium:*** 335 mg / ***Protein:*** 4.6 g

Flavors and taste:

This bread is filled with goodness, crunchy crust paired with a rich whole grain texture and taste.

Ingredients:

	1 Pound loaf	**1 ½ Pound loaf**	**2 Pound loaf**
Milk, warmed	½ cup	1 cup	1 ⅓ cups
Unsalted butter	2 tbsp	3 tbsp	4 tbsp
Plain bread flour	1 ½ cups	2 ¼ cups	3 cups
Multigrain cereal	½ cup	¾ cup	1 cup
Granulated brown sugar	¼ cup	⅔ cup	½ cup
Salt	¾ tsp	1 ⅛ tsp	1 ½ tsp
Bread machine yeast	¾ tsp	1 ⅛ tsp	1 ½ tsp

Directions:

1. Add the ingredients into the bread machine as per the order of the ingredients listed above or follow your bread machine's instruction manual.
2. Select the basic setting and medium crust function.
3. When ready, turn the bread out onto a drying rack and allow it to cool, then serve.

Tip(s):

1. When the loaf is fresh out from the machine and still hot, brush the top generously with butter and press this into some extra crushed multigrain cereal.

Simple and Savory Mixed Seed Loaf

Time: 3 hours and 5 minutes / **Prep Time:** 5 minutes / **Cook Time:** 3 hours

Nutritional facts per slice:

Calories: 196.7 *kcal* / *Total fat:* 4 *g* / *Saturated fat:* 0.6 *g* / *Cholesterol:* 0 *mg* / *Total carbohydrates:* 35 *g* / *Dietary fiber:* 2.8 *g* / *Sodium:* 293.1 *mg* / *Protein:* 5.6 *g*

Flavor and taste:

A great multiseed loaf for everyday use. It has a slight nutty taste to it, despite the lack of nuts. This bread tastes every bit as good as it smells!

Ingredients:

	1 Pound Loaf	1 ½ Pound Loaf	2 Pound Loaf
Lukewarm water	⅔ cup	1 cup	1 ⅓ cups
Salt	⅔ tsp	1 tsp	1 ⅓ tsp
Olive oil	1 tbsp and 1 tsp	2 tbsp	2 tbsp and 2 tsp
Whole wheat flour	⅔ cup	1 cup	1 and ⅓ cups
White bread flour	1 and ⅓ cups	2 cups	2 and ⅔ cups
Active dry yeast	1 tsp	1 ½ tsp	2 tsp
Linseed	2 tsp	3 tsp	4 ¼ tsp
Pumpkin seeds	2 tsp	3 tsp	4 ¼ tsp
Sesame seeds	2 tsp	3 tsp	4 ¼ tsp
Poppy seeds	2 tsp	3 tsp	4 ¼ tsp
Sunflower seeds	2 tsp	3 tsp	4 ¼ tsp

Directions:

1. Add all ingredients to your bread machine in the exact order listed. Seeds can be added in any order, as long as they come after the yeast.
2. Select the basic bread setting, along with any crust function you desire.
3. When ready, turn the bread out onto a drying rack so it can cool, then serve.

Tip(s):

1. When adding seeds for a 1 ½ pound loaf, the 5 seeds mixed together should fill a ⅓ cup. You can substitute these seeds for any other ⅓ cup of seed mix, but the ones in the recipe are my favorite for this bread.
2. Seed content for a 1 ½ pound loaf can be increased up to a ½ cup, but you must check your dough 10 minutes after kneading to ensure it has enough water.

NUT BREAD

Time: 3 hours and 15 minutes / **Prep Time:** 15 minutes / **Cook Time:** 3 hours

Nutrition Facts per slice:

Calories: 163 kcal / *Total fat:* 6.3 g / *Saturated fat:* 0.5 g / *Cholesterol:* 0 mg / *Total carbohydrates:* 22.8 g / *Dietary fiber:* 2.3 g / *Sodium:* 198 mg / *Protein:* 5.3 g

Flavors and taste:

A healthy alternative for the whole family. This nut bread has a wonderful, balanced texture, and the nuts bring a welcome crunchiness. I especially love eating this bread with a smear of honey.

Ingredients:

	1 Pound loaf	1 ½ Pound loaf	2 Pound loaf
Lukewarm water	⅔ cup	1 ¼ cup	1 ⅔ cup
Vegetable oil	½ tbsp	1 tbsp	1 ⅓ tbsp
Lemon juice	½ tsp	1 tsp	1 ⅓ tsp
Salt	1 tsp	1 ½ tsp	2 tsp
Molasses	⅙ cup	¼ cup	⅓ cup
Quick oatmeal	⅓ cup	½ cup	⅔ cup
Whole wheat flour	½ cup	1 cup	1 ⅓ cup
Plain bread flour	1 ⅓ cup	2 cups	2 ⅔ cups
Walnuts	1 ½ cups	¾ cup	1 cup
Instant dry yeast	1 ½ tsp	2 ¼ tsp	3 tsp

Directions:

1. Add the ingredients into the bread machine as per the order of the ingredients listed above or follow your bread machine's instruction manual.
2. Select the basic setting and soft crust function.
3. When ready, turn the bread out onto a drying rack and allow it to cool, then serve.

Tip(s):

1. For a difference in flavor, swap out the walnuts for sliced almonds or mixed nuts.
2. The molasses may be substituted with honey.

ALMOND AND DATES SWEET BREAD

Time: 3 hours and 10 minutes / **Prep Time:** 10 minutes / **Cook Time:** 3 hours

Nutritional facts per slice:

Calories: 112 *kcal* / *Total fat:* 4.2 *g* / *Saturated fat:* 0.5 *g* / *Cholesterol:* 0 *mg* / *Total carbohydrates:* 17.3 *g* / *Dietary fiber:* 2.5 *g* / *Sodium:* 98.1 *mg* / *Protein:* 2.9 *g*

Flavor and taste:

Most who try this bread say it's very sweet, although occasionally I'll find the rare sweet tooth who says it isn't sweet enough. It works well with peanut butter and jelly, and is delicious toasted!

Ingredients:

	1 Pound Loaf	1 ½ Pound Loaf	2 Pound Loaf
Lukewarm water	⅔ cup	1 cup	1 ½ cups
Vegetable oil	1 tbsp	1 ½ tbsp	2 tbsp and ¾ tsp
Honey	1 ⅓ tbsp	2 tbsp	3 tbsp
Salt	¼ tsp	½ tsp	¾ tsp
Rolled oats	½ cup	¾ cup	1 cup and 2 tbsp
Whole wheat flour	½ cup	1 ½ cups	2 cups
Bread flour	½ cup	1 ½ cups	2 cups
Active dry yeast	1 tsp	1 ½ tsp	2 ¼ tsp
Dates, chopped and pitted	⅓ cup	½ cup	¾ cup
Almonds, chopped	⅓ cup	½ cup	¾ cup

Directions:

1. Add all ingredients (except the dates and almonds) to the bread machine, either in the order listed, or according to your bread machine's instruction manual.
2. Select the nut and raisin setting, as well as the soft crust function.
3. Just before your bread machine enters its final kneading cycle (most machines will signal you with a beep around this time), add the dates and almonds.
4. When ready, turn the bread out onto a drying rack so it can cool, then serve.

Tip(s):

1. The dates can be swapped out with any dried fruit you desire.
2. For a chunkier date or fruit texture in your bread, throw the dates in 2 minutes before the bread is finished, rather than just before the final kneading cycle.

CHAPTER 10: SPECIAL BREADS

GLUTEN-FREE BREAD

Time: 2 hours and 50 minutes / **Prep Time:** 15 minutes / **Cook Time:** 2 hours and 35 minutes

Nutrition Facts per slice:

*Calories: 212 kcal / **Total fat:** 6g / **Saturated fat:** 3g / **Cholesterol:** 40 mg / **Total carbohydrates:** 35 g / **Dietary fiber:** 3 g **Sodium:** 263 mg / **Protein:** 5 g*

Flavors and taste:

Gluten-free bread is best served warm. This bread is soft and "*crumby*", much like the texture of a cake.

Ingredients:

	1 Pound loaf	**1 ½ Pound loaf**	**2 Pound loaf**
Lukewarm water	1 ⅛ cups	1 ⅕ cup	2 ¼ cups
Unsalted butter, diced	⅛ cup	¼ cup	⅓ cup
Egg	1 ½	2	3
Apple cider vinegar	¾ tsp	1 ⅛ tsp	1 ½ tsp
Honey	⅓ cup	½ cup	¾ cup
Gluten-free, all-purpose flour	2 ¼ cups	3 ⅓ cup	4 ½ cups
Salt	¾ tsp	1 ⅛ tsp	1 ½ tsp
Xanthan gum	1 ⅛ tsp	1 ½ tsp	2 ¼ tsp
Bread machine yeast	1 ⅛ tsp	1 ¾ tsp	2 ½ tsp

Directions:

1. Add the ingredients into the bread machine as per the order of the ingredients listed above or follow your bread machine's instruction manual.
2. Select the basic setting and soft crust function.
3. When ready, turn the bread out onto a drying rack and allow it to cool, then serve.

Tip(s):

1. If your bread maker has a gluten-free cycle, select that function instead of the basic setting.
2. Gluten-free flours differ, so it is important to make this bread using various brands to determine which one produces the best loaf.

NO SALT ADDED WHITE BREAD

Time: 3 hours and 10 minutes / **Prep Time:** 10 minutes / **Cook Time:** 3 hours

Nutrition Facts per slice:

Calories: 275.3 kcal / *Total fat:* 3 g / *Saturated fat:* 0.4 g / *Cholesterol:* 0 mg / *Total carbohydrates:* 52.9 g / *Dietary fiber:* 2 g / *Sodium:* 12.2 mg / *Protein:* 7.9 g

Flavors and taste:

This bread has a medium texture and, for a non-salted bread, has a wonderful taste.

Ingredients:

	1 Pound loaf	1 ½ Pound loaf	2 Pound loaf
Lukewarm water	½ cup	1 cup	1 ⅓ cups
Sugar	¾ tsp	1 ¼ tsp	1 ½ tsp
Instant dry yeast	¾ tsp	1 ¼ tsp	1 ½ tsp
White all-purpose flour	2 ⅛ cups	3 ¼ cups	4 ⅓ cups
Extra-virgin olive oil	½ tbsp	1 tbsp	1 ⅓ tbsp
Egg white	½	1	1 ⅓

Directions:

1. In a mixing bowl, combine the sugar and water. Stir until the sugar has dissolved then add in the yeast.
2. Add the flour, water mixture, and oil into the bread maker.
3. Select the French loaf setting and medium crust function.
4. Five minutes into the cycle, add in the egg white and allow the bread cycle to continue.
5. When ready, turn the bread out onto a drying rack and allow it to cool, then serve.

Tip(s):

1. The extra-virgin olive oil can be replaced with vegetable oils such as sunflower or canola.

Quinoa Bread

Time: 4 hours / **Prep Time:** 30 minutes / **Cook Time:** 3 hours and 30 minutes

Nutritional facts per slice:

Calories: 125 kcal / *Total fat:* 3.5 g / *Saturated fat:* 0.54 g / *Cholesterol:* 20 mg / *Total carbohydrates:* 20.44 g / *Dietary fiber:* 3.15 g / *Sodium:* 43 mg / *Protein:* 4.88 g

Flavor and taste:

A healthy bread with a pleasant, yet subtle, whole grain feel.

Ingredients:

	1 Pound Loaf	**1 ½ Pound Loaf**	**2 Pound Loaf**
Eggs	1, large	2, small	2, large
Olive oil	1 ½ tsp	2 ¼ tsp	1 tbsp
Whole wheat flour	1 ½ cups	2 ¼ cups	3 cups
Salt	2 pinches	3 pinches	¼ tsp
Pumpkin seeds	3 tsp	4 ½ tsp	6 tsp
Sunflower seeds	3 tsp	4 ½ tsp	6 tsp
Flax seeds	3 tsp	4 ½ tsp	6 tsp
Quinoa, cooked	½ cup	½ cup and 4 tbsp	1 cup
Lukewarm water	½ cup	½ cup and 4 tbsp	1 cup
Raw sugar	2 tbsp	1 tbsp and 1 tsp	¼ cup
Active dry yeast	¾ tsp	1 tsp and 2 pinches	1 ½ tsp

Directions:

1. Prepare your quinoa the way you'd cook standard rice: for every cup of quinoa, add 2 cups of water into a pot. Bring it to boil, then put the pot lid on and leave to simmer for 15-25 minutes.
2. Give the quinoa time to cool while you perform the rest of this recipe
3. In a separate container, add the lukewarm water, sugar and yeast. Stir, then let it sit as you continue onto step 4.
4. Begin adding the ingredients into your bread machine, either in the order listed, or according to your user manual. In case of conflict or uncertainty, the water/ sugar/ yeast mix should always go in last.
5. Select the whole wheat bread setting.
6. When ready, turn the bread out onto a drying rack so it can cool, then serve.

Tip(s):

1. Although it's always good practice to check your dough 10 minutes into its cycle, for this recipe you should always check it to see if it needs a little more water.

LOW-CARB KETO BREAD

Time: 3 hours and 15 minutes / **Prep Time:** 15 minutes / **Cook Time:** 3 hours

Nutrition Facts per slice:

*Calories: 122 kcal / **Total fat:** 5.4 g / **Saturated fat:** 1.4 g / **Cholesterol:** 72 mg / **Total carbohydrates:** 6.5 g / **Dietary fiber:** 2.4 g / **Sodium:** 158 mg / **Protein:** 13.3 g*

Flavors and taste:

This loaf of bread has a well-rounded flavor and is filling. This recipe is ideal for those who are seeking a low-carb option but love eating bread as much as I do!

Ingredients:

	1 Pound loaf	1 ½ Pound loaf	2 Pound loaf
Oat fiber	¼ cup	⅓ cup	½ cup
Flaxseed meal	⅓ cup	½ cup	⅔ cup
Wheat gluten	½ cup	1 cup	1 ¼ cup
Salt	½ tsp	¾ tsp	1 tsp
Xylitol	⅛ cup	⅙ cup	¼ cup
Xanthan gum	¼ tsp	⅓ tsp	½ tsp
Lukewarm water	½ cup	¾ cup	1 cup
Egg	1	1 ½	2
Honey	½ tsp	¾ tsp	1 tsp
Unsalted butter, softened	1 tbsp	1 ½ tbsp	2 tbsp
Active dry yeast	½ tbsp	¾ tbsp	1 tbsp

Directions:

1. In a mixing bowl, combine the oat fiber, meal, gluten, salt, xylitol, and xanthan gum.
2. Add the water, egg, honey, and butter into the bread machine, followed by the oat fiber mixture and yeast.
3. Select the basic setting and soft crust function.
4. When ready, turn the bread out onto a drying rack and allow it to cool, then serve.

Tip(s):

1. Add in a sprinkle of dried herbs when combining the dry ingredients to boost the taste of the bread.

PALEO AND DAIRY-FREE BREAD

Time: 3 hours and 20 minutes / **Prep Time:** 20 minutes / **Cook Time:** 3 hours

Nutrition Facts per slice:

Calories: 142 kcal / *Total fat:* 6.3 g / *Saturated fat:* 1.8g / *Cholesterol:* 34.9 mg / *Total carbohydrates:* 15.5 g / *Dietary fiber:* 4.4 g / *Sodium:* 236.8 mg / *Protein:* 4.1 g

Flavors and taste:

This is a moist bread with a texture that is similar to your standard whole wheat bread. The seeds inside the bread provide a welcome chewiness.

Tip(s):

1. The thicker the chia and flax meal mixture becomes, the more it will benefit your bread and provide the elasticity it needs to bake.

Ingredients:

	1 Pound loaf	1 ½ Pound loaf	2 Pound loaf
Flax meal	¼ cup	⅓ cup	½ cup
Chia seeds	2 tbsp	3 tbsp	4 tbsp
Coconut oil, melted	⅛ cup	⅙ cup	¼ cup
Egg	1 ½	2	3
Almond milk	¼ cup	⅓ cup	½ cup
Honey	½ tbsp	¾ tbsp	1 tbsp
Almond flour	1 cup	1 ½ cups	2 cups
Tapioca flour	⅔ cup	1 cup	1 ¼ cup
Coconut flour	⅛ cup	¼ cup	⅓ cup
Salt	½ tsp	¾ tsp	1 tsp
Cream of tartar	1 tsp	1 ½ tsp	2 tsp
Bread machine yeast	1 tsp	1 ½ tsp	2 tsp

Directions:

1. In a mixing bowl, combine one tablespoon of flax meal with the chia seeds. Stir in the water and set aside.

2. In a separate mixing bowl, pour in the melted coconut oil, eggs, almond milk, and honey. Whisk together. Followed by whisking in the flax meal and chia seed mixture. Pour this into the bread machine.

3. In a mixing bowl, combine the almond, tapioca, and coconut flour. Add the remainder of the flax meal and salt. Add in the cream of tartar and baking soda.

4. Pour the dry ingredients on top of the wet ingredients and finish by adding the yeast.

5. Select the whole wheat setting and medium crust function. When ready, turn the bread out onto a drying rack and allow it to cool, then serve.

CHAPTER 11:
FRUITY BREADS & CAKE

RAISIN BREAD

Time: 3 hours and 15 minutes / **Prep Time:** 15 minutes / **Cook Time:** 3 hours

Nutrition Facts per slice:

Calories: 78 kcal / ***Total fat:*** *1 g* / ***Saturated fat:*** *1 g* / ***Cholesterol:*** *3m g* / ***Total carbohydrates:*** *16 g* / ***Dietary fiber:*** *1 g* / ***Sodium:*** *106 mg* / ***Protein:*** *2 g*

Flavor and taste:

A lightly spiced, fruity bread that is not overpowering in flavor. Delectable, when served warm, straight out of the bread machine.

Ingredients:

	1 Pound loaf	**1 ½ Pound loaf**	**2 Pound loaf**
Lukewarm water	⅙ cup	1 cup	1 ⅓ cup
Unsalted butter, diced	1 ¼ tbsp	2 tbsp	2 ½ tbsp
Plain bread flour	2 cups	3 cups	4 cups
Orange zest	1 pinch	¼ tsp	⅓ tsp
Ground cinnamon	1 ⅓ tsp	2 tsp	2 ½ tsp
Ground clove	1 pinch	¼ tsp	⅓ tsp
Ground nutmeg	1 pinch	¼ tsp	⅓ tsp
Salt	1 pinch	1 tsp	1 ⅓ tsp
Sugar	1 ¼ tbsp	2 tbsp	2 ½ tbsp
Active dry yeast	1 ½ tsp	2 ¼ tsp	3 tsp
Raisins	½ cup	¾ cup	1 cup

Directions:

1. Add the ingredients into the bread machine as per the order of the ingredients listed above or follow your bread machine's instruction manual. Do not add the raisins in yet.
2. Select the nut or raisin setting and medium crust function.
3. When the machine signals you to add the raisins, do so.
4. When ready, turn the bread out onto a drying rack and allow it to cool, then serve.

Tip(s):

1. For extra taste, add mixed raisins instead of one variety.
2. You can select the basic setting with a medium crust function, and add the raisins in after the first phase of kneading has finished if your machine doesn't give you an "add-in" warning.

ORANGE CAKE LOAF

Time: 1 hour and 50 minutes / **Prep Time:** 5 minutes / **Cook Time:** 1 hour and 45 minutes

Nutritional facts per slice:

Calories: 247 *kcal* / ***Total fat:*** *4 g* / ***Saturated fat:*** *2 g* / ***Cholesterol:*** *39 mg* / ***Total carbohydrates:*** *49 g* / ***Dietary fiber:*** *1 g* / ***Sodium:*** *43 mg* / ***Protein:*** *4 g*

Flavor and taste:

Delightfully citrussy, this cake makes for a tangy dessert, tea, or even breakfast treat.

Ingredients:

	1 Pound Loaf	**1 ½ Pound Loaf**	**2 Pound Loaf**
Orange juice, room temperature	½ cup	⅔ cup	1 cup
Butter, softened	2 tbsp	3 tbsp	4 tbsp
Large egg, slightly beaten	1	2	3
Sugar	½ cup	1 cup	1 ½ cup
Dry milk powder	1 tbsp	1 ½ tbsp	2 tbsp
Corn starch	½ cup	¾ cup	1 cup
All-purpose flour	1 ½ cups	2 ¼ cups	3 cups
Baking powder	1 tbsp	1 ½ tbsp	2 tbsp

Ingredients for glaze topping:

Orange juice	1 tbsp	1 ½ tbsp	2 ¼ tbsp
Icing sugar	2 tbsp	3 tbsp and 1 tsp	¼ cup

Directions:

1. Place all ingredients (except the baking powder and glaze topping components) into the bread machine, either in the order given, or according to your bread machine's instruction manual
2. Select the cake cycle.
3. After 6 minutes, open the machine's lid and use a spatula to remove flour from the bread pan's sides. Do not remove anything from the bread machine as you do this; this includes the pan itself.
4. Close the lid and let the machine continue.
5. A further 4 minutes later (10 minutes after beginning), add the baking powder, as well as additional flour or orange juice, if necessary.
6. When ready, gently turn your loaf onto a clean tray or cooking surface.
7. Mix your glaze and pour it over your loaf while it is still hot, then leave it to cool.

Tip(s):

1. The butter can be swapped out for margarine.

FRUITY HARVEST BREAD

Time: 3 hours and 10 minutes / **Prep Time:** 10 minutes / **Cook Time:** 3 hours

Nutrition Facts per slice:

Calories: 214 kcal / *Total fat:* 6 g / *Saturated fat:* 2 g / *Cholesterol:* 25 mg / *Total carbohydrates:* 36 g / *Dietary fiber:* 2 g / *Sodium:* 330 mg / *Protein:* 6 g

Flavor and taste:

Savor while warm and fresh out of the bread machine or toasted with a smear of butter. This bread almost feels celebratory, with all its warm flavors. It is ideal for enjoying during fall and winter.

Ingredients:

	1 Pound loaf	**1 ½ Pound loaf**	**2 Pound loaf**
Egg	½ cup	1 egg	1 egg
Lukewarm water	½ cup	1 cup	1 ⅓ cup
Unsalted butter, softened	2 tbsp	3 tbsp	4 tbsp
Plain bread flour	2 ½ cups	3 ¾ cups	5 cups
Sugar	⅙ cup	¼ cup	⅓ cup
Salt	1 tsp	1 ½ tsp	2 tsp
Ground allspice	1 pinch	1 pinch	½ teaspoon
Ground nutmeg	1 pinch	1 pinch	½ teaspoon
Active dry yeast	1 ⅛ cup	2 tsp	2 ½ tsp
Pecan nuts, diced	¼ cup	⅓ cup	½ cup
Mixed dried fruit	½ cup	1 cup	1 ⅓ cup

Directions:

1. Add the ingredients into the bread machine as per the order of the ingredients listed above or follow your bread machine's instruction manual. Do not add in the nuts or fruit yet.
2. Select the nut or raisin setting and medium crust function.
3. When the machine beeps, signaling you to add the mixed dried fruit and nuts, do so.
4. When ready, turn the bread out onto a drying rack and allow it to cool, then serve.

Tip(s):

1. You can select the basic setting with a medium crust function, add the dried mixed fruit and nuts after the first phase of kneading has finished.

Eggless Vanilla Loaf

Time: 1 hour and 20 minutes / **Prep Time:** 5 minutes / **Cook Time:** 1 hour and 25 minutes

Nutritional facts per slice:

Calories: 317 *kcal* / *Total fat:* 12.3 *g* / *Saturated fat:* 3 *g* / *Cholesterol:* 11 *mg* / *Total carbohydrates:* 46.1 *g* / *Dietary fiber:* 0.9 *g* / *Sodium:* 159 *mg* / *Protein:* 5.9 *g*

Flavor and taste:

Moist and fluffy, this "plain" cake loaf is best cut into slices and smeared with butter, syrup, or honey.

Ingredients:

	1 Pound Loaf	1 ½ Pound Loaf	2 Pound Loaf
Lukewarm water	½ cup	1 cup	1 ½ cups
Olive oil	⅓ cup	½ cup	¾ cup
Vinegar	1 tsp	1 ½ tsp	2 ¼ tsp
Sweetened condensed milk	7 oz	14 oz	21 oz
Vanilla extract	1 tsp	1 ½ tsp	2 tsp
Sugar	2 tbsp	4 tbsp	6 tbsp
Salt	1 pinch	1 pinch	2 pinches
All-purpose flour	1 ½ cups	3 cups	4 ½ cups
Baking soda	½ tsp	1 tsp	1 ½ tsp
Baking powder	½ tsp	1 tsp	1 ½ tsp

Directions:

1. Add all ingredients into the bread machine, either in the order given or according to your machine's manufacturer, which would be preferable.
2. Select the cake cycle.
3. About 6 minutes in, use a spatula to scrape any flour residue on the sides of your machine into the mixture.
4. After the cake cycle, poke the loaf with a knife. If the knife has batter on it coming out, select the *bake* (often indicated with a "b") cycle and let it run for 5 minutes.
5. When your knife comes out clean, your bread is baked.
6. After 15-20 minutes of cooling in the machine, tip your loaf onto a drying rack to cool off further, then serve.

Tip(s):

1. The oil can be substituted for butter.
2. Any glaze works well with vanilla cake.

Mardi Gras King Cake

Serving Size: 14 servings

Time: 3 hours and 25 minutes / **Prep Time:** 20 minutes / **Cook Time:** 3 hours and 5 minutes

Flavor and taste:

Moist and decadent, this cake takes a little extra effort to make, but is well worth it. Truly the king among celebration cakes!

Ingredients:

- ¼ cup warm water
- 2 tbsp butter, softened
- 1, large egg, slightly beaten
- 1 cup sour cream
- 3 ½ tbsp white sugar
- ½ tsp salt
- 3 ½ cups all-purpose flour
- 2 ½ tsp active dry yeast

Ingredients for spread:

- ¼ cup and 1 tbsp white sugar
- 1 tsp cinnamon, ground
- 2 ½ tbsp butter, melted
- ½ cup pecan nuts, chopped

Ingredients for glaze topping:

- 2 cups icing sugar
- 1 ½ tbsp butter, melted
- 12 drops vanilla extract
- 2 tbsp milk
- 1 tbsp sugar, green-colored
- 1 tbsp sugar, sugar, yellow-colored
- 1 tbsp sugar, purple-colored

Directions:

1. Place the first 8 ingredients into the bread machine, either in the order listed, or according to the manufacturer.
2. Select the dough cycle.
3. Mix the first 3 spread ingredients in a bowl, and set aside.
4. Grease a baking sheet.
5. When the dough cycle ends, remove the dough, place it on a floured surface, and roll it out into a flat rectangle shape just under 10x28 inches.
6. Apply the spread to the flat dough surface and sprinkle the pecans over the dough evenly.
7. Pick up one of the length-sides of the dough, and roll it into a log just under 28 inches long.
8. Place dough log onto your greased baking sheet, seam-side down, and curve into a ring. Pinch the ends of the ring together so that they join. You may need to moisten the dough to do this.
9. Cover the ring with a cloth and leave to rise for 30 minutes.
10. When your loaf only has about 15 minutes left of rising, preheat your oven to 375 °F.
11. After rising, remove the cloth and place the cake in the oven until the top turns golden brown.
12. Mix the first 4 glaze ingredients together. Add or reduce milk to create a smooth, thick consistency.
13. When the cake is ready, remove from the oven and place on a drying rack. Apply glaze, and sprinkle colored sugar on top of the glazed cake in alternating bands.
14. Allow to cool completely before serving.

Tip(s):

1. Colored sugar can be made by mixing white sugar with food coloring.

Banana Bread

Time: 3 hours and 20 minutes / **Prep Time:** 20 minutes / **Cook Time:** 3 hours

Nutrition Facts per slice:

Calories: 194.7 kcal / *Total fat:* 7.3 g / *Saturated fat:* 1.9 g / *Cholesterol:* 50.6 mg / *Total carbohydrates:* 27.1 g / *Dietary fiber:* 2.2 g / *Sodium:* 4.2 g / *Protein:* 5.9 g

Flavor and taste:

This bread is soft and moist, with a ton of banana flavor in it. Delicious straight from the bread machine or toasted with a smear of butter.

Ingredients:

	1 Pound loaf	1 ½ Pound loaf	2 Pound loaf
Egg	2	3	4
Lukewarm 1% milk	¼ cup	¾ cup	½ cup
Unsalted butter, diced	⅓ cup	⅓ cup	½ cup
Banana	2	3	4
Plain bread flour	1 ⅓ cup	1 ¾ cup	2 ½ cup
Sugar/substitute	⅔ cup	1	1 ⅓ cup
Baking powder	1 ¼ tsp	1 ¾ tsp	2 ½ tsp
Baking soda	½ tsp	¾ tsp	1 tsp
Salt	½ tsp	¾ tsp	1 tsp
Mixed nuts, diced	½ cup	¾ cup	1 cup

Directions:

1. Put the eggs, milk, butter, and mashed banana into the bread machine in the exact order mentioned.
2. In a mixing bowl, combine the dry ingredients and nuts then transfer into the bread machine.
3. Select the quick setting and the soft crust function.
4. When ready, turn the bread out onto a drying rack and allow it to cool, then serve.

Tip(s):

1. When the machine finishes mixing the ingredients, be sure to scrape down the sides using a spatula to ensure that no pockets of flour form.
2. Bread machine settings vary, so check on your banana bread from time to time. You may need to remove the bread before the baking time has finished.
3. You can substitute butter for the same amount of applesauce.

APPLE CAKE

Serving Size: 10 servings

Time: 3 hours and 25 minutes / **Prep Time:** 25 minutes / **Cook Time:** 3 hours

Nutrition Facts per slice:

Calories: 480 *kcal* / *Total fat:* 10 *g* / *Saturated fat:* 5 *g* / *Cholesterol:* 25 *mg* / *Total carbohydrates:* 92 *g* / *Dietary fiber:* 3 *g* / *Sodium:* 710 *mg* / *Protein:* 8 *g*

Flavor and taste:

This is a wonderful recipe with honest flavors. Have a slice for breakfast or enjoy over afternoon tea.

Ingredients:

- ⅔ cup water
- 3 tbsp unsalted butter, softened
- 2 cups plain bread flour
- 3 tbsp granulated sugar
- 1 tsp salt
- 1 ½ tsp active dry yeast
- 1 can apple pie filling

Directions:

1. Add the ingredients into the bread machine as per the order of the ingredients listed above or follow your bread machine's instruction manual. Do not add the pie filling.
2. Select the dough setting.
3. Remove the dough and place it onto a floured surface. Cover with a cotton cloth for 15 minutes.
4. Roll the dough out into an even rectangular shape 13" x 8". Transfer this onto a greased baking tray. Fill the dough with the apple filling, running lengthwise. On each 13-inch side, make cuts from filling to edge of dough at 1-inch intervals, using a sharp knife. Fold ends of the dough up over the filling. Fold strips diagonally over filling, overlapping in the center and

alternating sides. Cover again with the cloth and allow to rest for 30 minutes or until the dough has doubled in size.
5. Preheat your oven to 375 °F and bake the cake for 40 minutes or until it has reached a beautiful golden color.
6. When ready, turn the apple cake out onto a drying rack and allow it to cool.
7. When cooled, dust with powdered sugar and serve.

Tip(s):
1. I added a few cloves to change the flavor of the apple pie filling. This a very versatile recipe, allowing you to add different pie fillings when you feel like it.
2. Instead of folding up the cake to form a pie, you can plait the bread too.

COFFEE CAKE

Serving Size: 1 standard cake

Time: 2 hours and 30 minutes / **Prep Time:** 1 hour / **Cook Time:** 1 hour and 30 minutes

Nutrition Facts per slice:

Calories: 313.1 *kcal* / *Total fat:* 11.1 g / *Saturated fat:* 4 g / *Cholesterol:* 35.9 *mg* / *Total carbohydrates:* 48.5 g / *Dietary fiber:* 2 g / *Sodium:* 344.1 *mg* / *Protein:* 5.9 g

Flavor and taste:

Everybody loves something sweet and this cake delivers. The spices in this cake bring extra warmth and the nuts bring some crunch. Enjoy with a strong cup of coffee or freshly brewed pot of tea.

Ingredients:

- Yolk of one egg
- ¾ cup whole milk
- 1 tbsp unsalted butter, melted
- 2 ¼ cups plain bread flour
- ¼ cup sugar
- 1 tsp salt
- 2 tsp active dry yeast

Ingredients for glaze topping:

- ¼ cup pecan nuts
- ¼ cup walnuts
- 1 tsp ground cinnamon
- ½ cup sugar
- 2 tbsp unsalted butter, melted

Directions:

1. Add the ingredients into the bread machine as per the order of the ingredients listed above or follow your bread machine's instruction manual.
2. Select the dough setting.
3. Prepare a 8 x 8" baking pan by greasing it.
4. When the dough cycle is finished, transfer the cake dough into the greased baking pan.
5. For the topping, glaze the two tablespoons of melted butter over the top.
6. In a small mixing bowl, combine the nuts, sugar, and cinnamon and sprinkle over the top of the cake dough.
7. Cover the cake dough with a cloth and allow to rest in a warm area for 30 minutes.
8. Preheat your oven to 375 °F and bake the cake for 20 minutes or until it has turned a golden color.
9. When ready, turn the bread out onto a drying rack and allow it to cool, then serve.

Tip(s):

1. For an extra kick of decadence combine 1 cup powdered sugar, ½ teaspoon vanilla essence, 1 teaspoon unsalted butter, melted, 2 tablespoons whole milk and 1 cup powdered sugar. Drizzle this over the cake when you remove it from the oven.

CHAPTER 12:
ROLLS & PIZZA

"Po Boy" Rolls from New Orleans

Serving Size: 6 rolls

Time: 50 minutes (excluding the rising time of 1 hour and 30 minutes) / **Prep Time:** 25 minutes / **Cook Time:** 25 minutes

Nutrition Facts per serving:

Calories: 280 kcal / *Total fat:* 3.5 g / *Saturated fat:* 0 g / *Cholesterol:* 0 g / *Total carbohydrates:* 52 g / *Dietary fiber:* 2 g / *Sodium:* 600 mg / *Protein:* 8 g

Flavor and taste:

These rolls are crispy on the outside and light and fluffy on the inside. Perfect for sandwiches or soaking up soup and stews.

Ingredients:

- 1 cup water
- 1 tbsp granulated sugar
- 1 ½ tsp salt
- 1 tbsp extra-virgin olive oil
- 3 cups plain bread flour
- 1 tbsp instant dry yeast

Directions:

1. Add the ingredients into the bread machine as per the order of the ingredients listed above or follow your bread machine's instruction manual.
2. Select the dough setting.
3. When the dough is ready, place it onto a floured surface and split it into six even pieces. Then transfer them onto a parchment-lined baking tray.
4. Switch on the oven for 2 minutes, then turn it off. Place the dough into the oven and allow it to rise for one hour and 30 minutes or until it has doubled in size then remove.
5. Preheat your oven to 400 °F and then place an oven-proof dish on the lowest rack.
6. Using a sharp knife make slashes into the dough and mist with water.
7. When the oven has reached 400°F, place the dough into the oven and bake for 20 minutes or until the rolls, have reached a golden color.
8. When ready, turn the bread out onto a drying rack and allow it to cool, then serve.

Tip(s):

1. If you plan to use the dough the following day, remove the dough the minute the machine has finished its kneading cycle. Place into an oiled bowl and cover tightly with cling wrap, storing in the refrigerator overnight.

100% WHOLE WHEAT DINNER ROLLS

Time: 2 hours and 20 minutes / **Prep Time:** 5 minutes / **Cook Time:** 2 hours and 15 minutes

Nutritional facts per slice:

Calories: 196 *kcal* / *Total fat:* 8 *g* / *Saturated fat:* 4 *g* / *Cholesterol:* 58 *mg* / *Total carbohydrates:* 26 *g* / *Dietary fiber:* 3 *g* / *Sodium:* 222 *mg* / *Protein:* 6 *g*

Flavor and taste:

An alternative 100% whole wheat recipe, now in roll form. Very soft, and goes well with ham and cheese.

Ingredients:

	8 Rolls	12 Rolls	18 Rolls
Warm milk	½ cup	¾ cup	1 cup and 2 tbsp
Butter, melted	¼ cup	⅓ cup	½ cup
Large egg, lightly beaten	2	3	4
Sugar	2 tbsp	4 tbsp	6 tbsp
Salt	½ tsp	¾ tsp	1 tsp and 2 pinches
Whole wheat flour	2 cups	3 cups	4 ½ cups
Instant yeast	1 ½ tsp	2 ¼ tsp	4 tsp

Directions:
1. Place all ingredients into your bread machine, either in the order listed, or according to your manufacturer.
2. Select the dough setting.
3. When the dough cycle finishes, remove your dough from the bread pan.
4. Split dough into 18/12/8 balls.
5. Place balls onto a greased pan, with 1 inch of space between them.
6. Cover balls with a cloth and let rise for 45 minutes. Do not put them in the oven yet.
7. When 15 minutes of rising remains, preheat the oven to 350 °F.
8. When fully risen, remove the cloth and place the balls in the oven. Let them bake until they turn a light golden-brown color; this takes about 20 minutes.
9. Remove from the oven, and allow to cool before serving.

Tip(s):
1. Adding a light layer of flour to your ball-rolling surface can prevent residue sticking to countertops.

CLASSIC DINNER ROLLS

Serving Size: 15 rolls

Time: 3 hours / **Prep Time:** 25 minutes / **Cook Time:** 2 hours and 35 minutes

Nutrition Facts per serving:

Calories: 135 *kcal* / *Total fat:* 2 *g* / *Saturated fat:* 0 *g* / *Cholesterol:* 15 *mg* / *Total carbohydrates:* 26 *g* / *Dietary fiber:* 1 *g* / *Sodium:* 170 *mg* / *Protein:* 4 *g*

Flavor and taste:

Super fluffy and light dinner rolls.

Ingredients:
- 1 egg
- 1 cup water
- 3 ¼ cups plain bread flour
- ¼ cup sugar
- 1 tsp salt
- 3 tsp active dry yeast
- 2 tbsp unsalted butter, softened

Directions:
1. Add the ingredients into the bread machine as per the order of the ingredients listed above or follow your bread machine's instruction manual. Do not add the softened butter in.
2. Select the dough setting.
3. Transfer the dough onto a floured surface and allow to rest for 10 minutes. Then split the dough evenly into 15 balls.
4. On a greased baking tray, place the dough balls 2" apart. Allow the rolls to rest in a warm area for 30 minutes or until they have doubled in size.
5. Preheat your oven to 375 °F and bake the rolls for 15 minutes or until they have turned a honeyed color.
6. Brush the tops of the rolls with the softened butter, then serve.

Tip(s):
1. Place the rolls closely together if you enjoy your rolls with softer sides.
2. If you cover the dough rolls with cling wrap, they can keep for two days in the refrigerator.

Vegan Dinner Rolls

Time: 2 hours and 20 minutes / **Prep Time:** 10 minutes / **Cook Time:** 2 hours and 10 minutes

Nutritional facts per slice:

Calories: 110 *kcal* / *Total fat:* 2.3 *g* / *Saturated fat:* 0.8 *g* / *Cholesterol:* 0 *mg* / *Total carbohydrates:* 19.6 *g* / *Dietary fiber:* 0.7 *g* / *Sodium:* 135 *mg* / *Protein:* 2.4 *g*

Flavor and taste:

These rolls are soft and fluffy, and go really well with butter and jam.

Ingredients:

	8 Rolls	**12 Rolls**	**18 Rolls**
Lukewarm water	2 ⅔ tbsp	¼ cup	⅜ cup (6 tbsp)
Almond milk, unsweetened	⅓ tsp	½ cup	¾ cup
Vegan butter, softened or melted	1 ⅓ tbsp	2 tbsp	3 tbsp
Organic cane sugar	1 ⅓ tbsp	2 tbsp	3 tbsp
Salt	⅓ tsp	½ tsp	¾ tsp
Unbleached all-purpose flour	1 ⅓ cups	2 cups	3 cups
Instant yeast	1 ½ tsp	2 ¼ tsp	3 ½ tsp

Directions:

1. Add all ingredients to your bread machine, either in the order listed, or according to your manufacturer.
2. Select the dough setting.
3. When the cycle finishes, remove your dough from the pan.
4. Split dough into 18/12/8 balls.
5. Place balls onto a greased pan, with 1 inch of space between them.
6. Cover balls with a cloth and allow to rise for 45 minutes.
7. Preheat the oven to 375 °F when about 15 minutes of rising remains.
8. When the bread has fully risen, place the balls in the oven and let them bake until they turn a light golden-brown color. This takes about 20 minutes.
9. Remove from the oven, and allow to cool before serving.

Tip(s):

1. "Earth Balance" brand vegan butter can be purchased from Publix or Kroger.
2. Up to ⅓ of the total flour can be substituted with whole wheat.

Buttery Dinner Rolls

Time: 2 hours and 20 minutes / **Prep Time:** 10 minutes / **Cook Time:** 2 hours and 10 minutes

Nutritional facts per slice:

Calories: 170 kcal / *Total fat:* 6 g / *Saturated fat:* 3 g / *Cholesterol:* 33 mg / *Total carbohydrates:* 23 g / *Dietary fiber:* 2 g / *Sodium:* 156 mg / *Protein:* 5 g

Flavor and taste:

These are the best buttery buns for any dinner occasion!

Ingredients:

	8 Rolls	**12 Rolls**	**18 Rolls**
Milk, warm	½ cup	⅔ cup	1 cup
Butter, softened	¼ cup	⅓ cup	½ cup
White sugar	2 tbsp	3 tbsp	¼ cup
Eggs	1, large	2, small	2, large
Salt	⅓ tsp	½ tsp	¾ tsp
Whole wheat flour	1 ⅓ cups	2 cups	3 cups
All-purpose flour	7 tbsp	⅔ cup	1 cup
Instant yeast	1 tsp	2 tsp	3 tsp

Directions:

1. Add all ingredients to your bread machine in the exact order listed.
2. Select the dough setting.
3. When the cycle finishes, remove dough from pan.
4. Split dough into 18/12/8 balls. Place them onto a greased pan, with 1 inch of space between them.
5. Cover balls with a cloth and allow to rise for 45 minutes.
6. Preheat the oven to 350 °F when about 15 minutes of rising remains.
7. When the bread has fully risen, place the balls in the oven and let them bake until they turn a light golden-brown color. This takes about 20 minutes.
8. Remove from oven, and allow to cool before serving.

Tip(s):

1. 5 minutes into the dough cycle, check for dryness. For this recipe, it's best to err on the wet side, and risk adding too much extra milk rather than too little.
2. Splitting dough into fewer, larger balls is possible, but will increase baking time.

Cinnamon Rolls

Serving Size: 18 rolls

Time: 3 hours and 18 minutes / **Prep Time:** 3 hours / **Cook Time:** 18 minutes

Nutrition Facts per serving:

Calories: 346 kcal / *Total fat:* 11.7 g / *Saturated fat:* 5.2 g / *Cholesterol:* 39.3 mg / *Total carbohydrates:* 56.6 g / *Dietary fiber:* 1.4 g / *Sodium:* 138.3 mg / *Protein:* 4.4 g

Flavor and taste:

Warm, rich cinnamon flavors with a sweet finish, who does not love a cinnamon roll?

Ingredients for filling:

- 1 cup brown sugar
- ½ cup unsalted butter, softened
- 1 ½ tbsp ground cinnamon

Ingredients for icing:

- 4 tbsp whole milk
- ½ tsp vanilla essence
- 2 tbsp unsalted butter, melted
- 3 cups powdered sugar

Ingredients for dough:

- 1 ⅓ cups lukewarm water
- 1 tbsp unsalted butter, diced
- 5 tbsp sugar
- 1 egg
- 1 tsp salt
- 3 cups white all-purpose flour
- 1 ½ cups plain bread flour
- ¼ cup powdered milk
- 1 tbsp dry active yeast

Directions:

1. Add the dough ingredients into the bread machine as per the order of the ingredients listed above or follow your bread machine's instruction manual.
2. Select the dough setting.
3. Place the dough onto a floured surface and split into two portions.
4. Roll one of the portions into a rectangular shape.
5. Combine the ingredients for the filling, and spread half of it evenly over the rolled-out piece of dough.
6. Using a sharp knife, cut the dough into 1" wide strips. Then roll up to form pinwheels.
7. Place these pinwheels onto a greased baking tray.
8. Repeat the same process above with the remaining portion of dough and remaining ingredients for the filling.
9. Cover the pinwheels with a cloth and allow to rise for 30 minutes.
10. Preheat the oven to 375 °F and bake the cinnamon rolls for 18 minutes.
11. Mix the ingredients for the icing together and spread this over the top of the warm cinnamon rolls, then serve.

Tip(s):

1. When the rolls are baking, you can test if they are ready by tapping your fingers in the middle. If the dough bounces back a little, then they are ready.

Pizza Dough Recipe

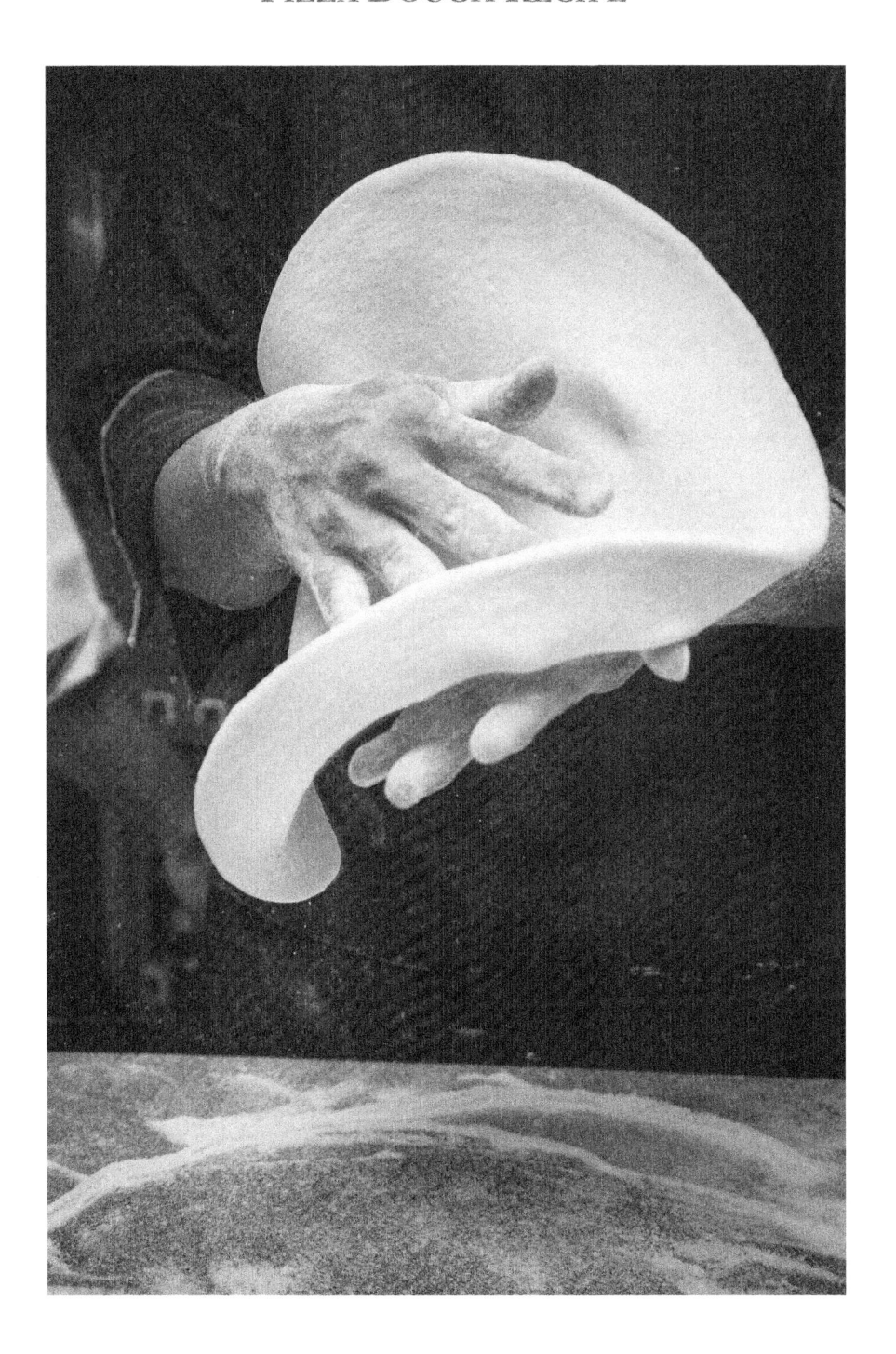

Serving Size: 6 servings

Time: 1 hour and 45 minutes / **Prep Time:** 15 minutes / **Cook Time:** 1 hour and 30 minutes

Nutrition Facts per pizza base (without toppings):

Calories: 536 kcal / *Total fat:* 7 g / *Saturated fat:* 4 g / *Cholesterol:* 15 mg / *Total carbohydrates:* 102 g / *Dietary fiber:* 4 g / *Sodium:* 1221 mg / *Protein:* 14 g

Flavor and taste:

A simple recipe for pizza dough that sees that you never order in pizza again. This is a wonderful way to get the little ones involved, from adding the ingredients to the machine to adding their own toppings.

Ingredients:

- 2 cups plain bread flour
- 1 tbsp unsalted butter, softened
- 1 tbsp sugar
- 1 tsp instant dry yeast
- 1 tsp salt
- ½ cup lukewarm water

Directions:

1. Add the ingredients into the bread machine as per the order of the ingredients listed above or follow your bread machine's instruction manual.
2. Select the dough setting and press start.
3. Ten minutes into the bread machine's cycle, check on the dough to ensure that the ingredients have mixed evenly and that the dough is not too wet or dry.
4. Preheat your oven to 400 °F.
5. When ready, turn the dough out onto a floured surface and knead into a pizza or pan dish shape.
6. Top with your desired toppings and bake for 20 to 25 minutes.

Tip(s):

1. For those like me who like a crust that is a tad crunchier, brush the pizza base with a bit of extra-virgin olive oil before placing it into the oven.
2. Double the ingredients to create two standard size pizza bases.

CHAPTER 13: ASSORTED PARTY RECIPES

BREADSTICKS

Time: 2 hours and 15 minutes / **Prep Time:** 5 minutes / **Cook Time:** 2 hours and 10 minutes

Nutritional facts per slice:

Calories: 196 kcal / *Total fat:* 8 g / *Saturated fat:* 4 g / *Cholesterol:* 58 mg / *Total carbohydrates:* 26 g / *Dietary fiber:* 3 g / *Sodium:* 222 mg / *Protein:* 6 g

Flavor and taste:

These breadsticks have an outstanding crispy texture with a soft center. You'll never need to scavenge for Olive Garden copycats again!

Ingredients:

	8 Breadsticks	12 Breadsticks	16 Breadsticks
Lukewarm water	⅔ cup	1 cup	1 ⅓ cups
Butter, softened	½ tbsp	2 ¼ tsp	1 tbsp
Sugar	¾ tbsp	1 tbsp and ⅓ tsp	1 ½ tbsp
Salt	¾ tsp	1 tsp and 2 pinches	1 ½ tsp
Plain bread flour	2 cups	3 cups	4 cups
Instant yeast	1 tsp	1 ½ tsp	2 tsp

Ingredients for glaze topping:

Water	½ tbsp	2 ¼ tsp	1 tbsp
Egg whites	1, small	1, small	1, large

Directions:

1. Add all non-glaze ingredients into your bread machine in the exact order given.
2. Select the dough cycle.
3. When the cycle completes, empty your dough onto a lightly floured countertop.
4. Split dough into 16/12/8 balls.
5. Stretch each ball into a 6-8-inch rope.
6. Place on a baking sheet. No grease required.
7. Preheat the oven to 400 °F.
8. Cover with a cloth and allow 20 minutes for the dough ropes to rise.
9. Mix your glaze ingredients together, then brush your ropes after they've risen.
10. After this, remove the cloth and place the balls in the oven to bake until they turn a light golden-brown color. This takes about 10-15 minutes.
11. Remove from the oven, and allow to cool before serving.

Tip(s):

1. While glazing, feel free to add coarse salt or fine seeds to the top of your dough ropes for extra crunch and flavor once they're done.

Texas Roadhouse-Style Glazed Buns

Time: 2 hours and 5 minutes / **Prep Time:** 5 minutes / **Cook Time:** 2 hours

Flavor and taste:

These are absolutely delicious, even without the glaze. Already sweet to start with, I love to smear mine with extra honey or butter before serving for maximum indulgence.

Ingredients:

	1 Pound Batch	1 ½ Pound Batch	2 Pound Batch
Lukewarm water	¼ cup	8 tsp	¼ cup
Lukewarm milk	½ cup	⅔ cup	1 cup
Salt	½ tsp	⅔ tsp	1 tsp
Butter, softened	¾ tbsp	1 tbsp	1 ½ tbsp
Egg	1, small	1, small	1, large
Sugar	2 tbsp	2 ½ tbsp	¼ cup
Plain bread flour	1 ¾ cup	2 ⅓ cups	3 ½ cups
Active dry yeast	1 tsp	1 ½ tsp	2 ¼ tsp

Ingredients for glaze topping:

	1 Pound Batch	1 ½ Pound Batch	2 Pound Batch
Salted butter, softened	¼ cup	⅓ cup	½ cup
Icing sugar	2 ½ tbsp	3 ½ tbsp	⅓ cup
Cinnamon, ground	½ tsp	⅔ tsp	1 tsp

Directions:

1. Place all non-glaze ingredients into the bread machine, either in the order listed, or according to your machine's manufacturer.
2. Select the dough setting.
3. Once finished, place the dough on a lightly floured countertop, and roll it into a rectangle that is half an inch thick.
4. Fold dough in half, cover with a cloth, and let it rest for 15 minutes.
5. Preheat oven to 350 °F.
6. While the oven heats, cut your dough into squares. 18 squares for a 2-pound batch, 12 squares for a 1 ½ pound batch, and 8 squares for a 1-pound batch.
7. On a baking tray, place your dough and put it in the oven until your buns start going golden-brown. This should take 10-15 minutes.
8. While your buns are baking, mix your glaze in a small bowl. Start by beating your butter, then slowly add in the icing sugar, then top it off with cinnamon, mixing well.
9. When your buns are ready, remove them from the oven, apply your glaze over the top of each bun with a spoon or knife while still hot. Can be served warm.

Tip(s):

1. You can further glaze your buns with honey for a sweeter flavor.

Chocolate Chip Banana Bread

Time: 2 hours and 5 minutes / **Prep Time:** 5 minutes / **Cook Time:** 2 hours

Nutritional facts per slice:

Calories: 262 kcal / *Total fat:* 11 g / *Saturated fat:* 4 g / *Cholesterol:* 42 mg / *Total carbohydrates:* 36 g / *Dietary fiber:* 1 g / *Sodium:* 212 mg / *Protein:* 4 g

Flavor and taste:

This recipe has all the goodness from the earlier banana bread recipe, but with a chocolatey addition that makes for great dessert bread.

Ingredients:

	1 Pound Loaf	1 ½ Pound Loaf	2 Pound Loaf
Large egg	1	2	3
Butter, melted	¼ cup	⅓ cup	½ cup
Milk	1 tbsp	2 tbsp	3 tbsp
Bananas, mashed	1	2	3
All-purpose flour	1 cup	2 cups	3 cups
Sugar	⅓ cup	⅔ cups	1 cup
Baking powder	1 tsp	1 ½ tsp	2 tsp
Baking soda	⅓ tsp	½ tsp	¾ tsp
Salt	⅓ tsp	½ tsp	¾ tsp
Walnuts, chopped	⅓ cup	½ cup	¾ cup
Chocolate chips	⅓ cup	½ cup	¾ cup

Directions:

1. Pour the first four ingredients into the bread pan.
2. In a separate bowl, mix the rest of the ingredients.
3. Pour the contents of the bowl into the bread pan.
4. Select the quick setting and the soft crust function, if applicable.
5. When ready, turn the bread out onto a drying rack and allow it to cool, then serve.

Tip(s):

1. To ensure your banana bread is done, stick it with a knife. If it comes out clean, it is ready. If not, set the bread for a bake setting and poke it periodically. When the knife comes out clean, it's done.

Cranberry and Cardamom Bread

Time: 2 hours and 5 minutes / **Prep Time:** 5 minutes / **Cook Time:** 2 hours

Nutritional facts per slice:

Calories: 124 kcal / *Total fat:* 1.8 g / *Saturated fat:* 1.4 g / *Cholesterol:* 0 mg / *Total carbohydrates:* 23.3 g / *Dietary fiber:* 1.3 g / *Sodium:* 196 mg / *Protein:* 3.1 g

Flavor and taste:

Sweet and roasted, this recipe goes well as toast, plain with butter, or even with meats.

Ingredients:

	1 Pound Loaf	1 ½ Pound Loaf	2 Pound Loaf
Lukewarm water	½ cup	1 cup	1 ½ cups
Brown sugar	1 tsbp	1 ½ tbsp	2 tbsp
Salt	½ tsp	1 tsp	1 ½ tsp
Coconut oil, melted	1 tbsp	1 ½ tbsp	2 tbsp
Plain bread flour	2 cups	3 cups	4 cups
Cinnamon	1 tsp	1 ½ tsp	2 tsp
Cardamom	1 tsp	1 ½ tsp	2 tsp
Cranberries, dried	½ cup	¾ cup	1 cup
Active dry yeast	1 tsp	1 ½ tsp	2 tsp

Directions:

1. Place all ingredients into your bread machine in the order listed.
2. Select the sweet bread setting.
3. When ready, turn the bread out onto a drying rack so it can cool, then serve.

Tip(s):

1. Be sure to always check this loaf 10 minutes after the machine begins running. It is prone to needing additional water or flour.

Chocolate Chip Brioche

Time: 2 hours and 45 minutes / **Prep Time:** 30 minutes / **Cook Time:** 2 hours and 15 minutes

Nutritional facts per slice:

Calories: 146 kcal / *Total fat:* 4 g / *Saturated fat:* 2 g / *Cholesterol:* 44 mg / *Total carbohydrates:* 23 g / *Dietary fiber:* 1 g / *Sodium:* 212 mg / *Protein:* 5 g

Flavor and taste:

Gentle, rich and divinely sweet; if I could marry this brioche, I would.

Ingredients:

	1 Pound Batch	1 ½ Pound Batch	2 Pound Batch
Lukewarm water	3 ½ tbsp	⅓ cup	½ cup
Lukewarm milk	3 ½ tbsp	⅓ cup	½ cup
Unsalted butter, softened	1 tbsp and 2 ⅓ tsp	2 ⅔ tbsp	4 tbsp
Egg	2, small	2, large	3, large
Sugar	1 ⅓ tbsp	2 tbsp	3 tbsp
All-purpose flour	1 ⅔ cups	2 ½ cups	3 ¾ cups
Salt	⅔ tsp	1 tsp	1 ½ tsp
Instant yeast	⅔ tsp	1 tsp	1 ½ tsp
Chocolate chips	⅔ cup	1 cup	1 ½ cups

Directions:

1. Place all ingredients, except the chocolate chips, into your bread machine in the order listed.
2. Select the dough setting.
3. Add the chocolate chips to the dough about 3 minutes before its final kneading cycle.
4. When done, place dough on countertop and split into balls. A 2-pound loaf should have 18 balls, a 1 ½ pound loaf should have 12 balls, and a 1-pound loaf should have 8 balls. Be gentle when forming them.
5. Cover with a deeply greased plastic wrap and let the balls rise in a warm room for 45 minutes.
6. Preheat your oven to 400 °F.
7. Once your balls have finished rising, place them on an oven rack until golden brown. This will take about 15 minutes.
8. When done, remove from oven and allow to cool on a drying rack. Then, serve.

Tip(s):

1. The dough for this recipe will be stickier than most of the others in this book. This is alright. Only add flour if it seems too thin and batter-like.
2. Brioche is best glazed. Apply whichever glaze you prefer between step 4 and 5 under the directions.
3. Traditional brioche uses a glaze made up of beaten egg and pearl sugar.
4. Be sure to give the balls room to breathe before placing them in the oven. Do not be alarmed if they touch as they heat up. This is normal, and means your brioche will form a lovely pull-apart bread when it is done.

CONCLUSION

With the selection of recipes mentioned in this book, I am sure there is a loaf of bread that will appeal to each family member, and suit everyone's tastes.

Baking bread using your bread machine is a rewarding experience. Soon, store-bought loaves will be replaced by your own creations. Never be afraid to get creative in the kitchen and add or omit ingredients to enhance and change the flavors of your bread.

There are so many wonderful, tasty bread recipes available, and I hope that this book inspires you to use the recipes and search for new ones to try. There are so many options available that you could find yourself baking a different bread each day.

Once you begin baking, the task will become easier. With this book, you will resolve any issues that may arise in the baking process.

The Nutrition Facts mentioned in the book are also there as a guide for those who are following healthy eating programs or for those who have specific health conditions. After all, it is important to know what is in each slice, and when it comes to eating oven-baked bread, it is always good to know if you can indulge in another slice. Who could resist?

The beauty of the humble bread machine is that you do not need a large kitchen to get started, as long as you have some space for it to stand and pour ingredients into, you are all set. This helpful little device makes baking a breeze and leaves the mess out of the picture.

Baking bread is not just a delicious and addictive hobby, but a way in which to stay away from all the *"bad"* ingredients that many store-bought varieties contain. Seeing your ingredients get to work to churn out a *"yummy"* bread is not just satisfying but allows you to also create a newfound family tradition, and to me, there is nothing better!

Printed in Great Britain
by Amazon